Film Music

Very Short Introductions available now:

AFRICAN HISTORY John Parker and Richard Rathbone
AMERICAN POLITICAL PARTIES AND ELECTIONS L. Sandy Maisel
THE AMERICAN PRESIDENCY Charles O. Jones
ANARCHISM Colin Ward
ANCIENT EGYPT Ian Shaw
ANCIENT PHILOSOPHY Julia Annas
ANCIENT WARFARE Harry Sidebottom
ANGLICANISM Mark Chapman
THE ANGLO-SAXON AGE John Blair
ANIMAL RIGHTS David DeGrazia
ANTISEMITISM Steven Beller
THE APOCRYPHAL GOSPELS Paul Foster
ARCHAEOLOGY Paul Bahn
ARCHITECTURE Andrew Ballantyne
ARISTOTLE Jonathan Barnes
ART HISTORY Dana Arnold
ART THEORY Cynthia Freeland
ATHEISM Julian Baggini
AUGUSTINE Henry Chadwick
AUTISM Uta Frith
BARTHES Jonathan Culler
BESTSELLERS John Sutherland
THE BIBLE John Riches
BIBLICAL ARCHEOLOGY Eric H. Cline
BIOGRAPHY Hermione Lee
THE BOOK OF MORMON Terryl Givens
THE BRAIN Michael O'Shea
BRITISH POLITICS Anthony Wright
BUDDHA Michael Carrithers
BUDDHISM Damien Keown
BUDDHIST ETHICS Damien Keown
CAPITALISM James Fulcher
CATHOLICISM Gerald O'Collins
THE CELTS Barry Cunliffe
CHAOS Leonard Smith
CHOICE THEORY Michael Allingham
CHRISTIAN ART Beth Williamson
CHRISTIANITY Linda Woodhead
CITIZENSHIP Richard Bellamy
CLASSICAL MYTHOLOGY Helen Morales
CLASSICS Mary Beard and John Henderson
CLAUSEWITZ Michael Howard
THE COLD WAR Robert McMahon
COMMUNISM Leslie Holmes
CONSCIOUSNESS Susan Blackmore
CONTEMPORARY ART Julian Stallabrass
CONTINENTAL PHILOSOPHY Simon Critchley
COSMOLOGY Peter Coles
THE CRUSADES Christopher Tyerman
CRYPTOGRAPHY Fred Piper and Sean Murphy
DADA AND SURREALISM David Hopkins
DARWIN Jonathan Howard
THE DEAD SEA SCROLLS Timothy Lim
DEMOCRACY Bernard Crick
DESCARTES Tom Sorell
DESERTS Nick Middleton
DESIGN John Heskett
DINOSAURS David Norman
DOCUMENTARY FILM Patricia Aufderheide
DREAMING J. Allan Hobson
DRUGS Leslie Iversen
THE EARTH Martin Redfern
ECONOMICS Partha Dasgupta
EGYPTIAN MYTH Geraldine Pinch

EIGHTEENTH-CENTURY BRITAIN Paul Langford
THE ELEMENTS Philip Ball
EMOTION Dylan Evans
EMPIRE Stephen Howe
ENGELS Terrell Carver
EPIDEMIOLOGY Roldolfo Saracci
ETHICS Simon Blackburn
THE EUROPEAN UNION John Pinder and Simon Usherwood
EVOLUTION Brian and Deborah Charlesworth
EXISTENTIALISM Thomas Flynn
FASCISM Kevin Passmore
FASHION Rebecca Arnold
FEMINISM Margaret Walters
FILM MUSIC Kathryn Kalinak
THE FIRST WORLD WAR Michael Howard
FORENSIC SCIENCE Jim Fraser
FOSSILS Keith Thomson
FOUCAULT Gary Gutting
FREE SPEECH Nigel Warburton
FREE WILL Thomas Pink
FRENCH LITERATURE John D. Lyons
THE FRENCH REVOLUTION William Doyle
FREUD Anthony Storr
FUNDAMENTALISM Malise Ruthven
GALAXIES John Gribbin
GALILEO Stillman Drake
GAME THEORY Ken Binmore
GANDHI Bhikhu Parekh
GEOGRAPHY John Matthews and David Herbert
GEOPOLITICS Klaus Dodds
GERMAN LITERATURE Nicholas Boyle
GLOBAL CATASTROPHES Bill McGuire
GLOBAL WARMING Mark Maslin
GLOBALIZATION Manfred Steger
THE GREAT DEPRESSION AND THE NEW DEAL Eric Rauchway
HABERMAS James Gordon Finlayson
HEGEL Peter Singer
HEIDEGGER Michael Inwood
HIEROGLYPHS Penelope Wilson
HINDUISM Kim Knott
HISTORY John H. Arnold
THE HISTORY OF ASTRONOMY Michael Hoskin
THE HISTORY OF LIFE Michael Benton
THE HISTORY OF MEDICINE William Bynum
THE HISTORY OF TIME Leofranc Holford-Strevens
HIV/AIDS Alan Whiteside
HOBBES Richard Tuck
HUMAN EVOLUTION Bernard Wood
HUMAN RIGHTS Andrew Clapham
HUME A. J. Ayer
IDEOLOGY Michael Freeden
INDIAN PHILOSOPHY Sue Hamilton
INFORMATION Luciano Floridi
INNOVATION Mark Dodgson and David Gann
INTELLIGENCE Ian J. Deary
INTERNATIONAL MIGRATION Khalid Koser
INTERNATIONAL RELATIONS Paul Wilkinson
ISLAM Malise Ruthven
ISLAMIC HISTORY Adam Silverstein
JOURNALISM Ian Hargreaves
JUDAISM Norman Solomon
JUNG Anthony Stevens
KABBALAH Joseph Dan
KAFKA Ritchie Robertson
KANT Roger Scruton

KIERKEGAARD Patrick Gardiner
THE KORAN Michael Cook
LAW Raymond Wacks
THE LAWS OF THERMODYNAMICS Peter Atkins
LINCOLN Allen C. Guelzo
LINGUISTICS Peter Matthews
LITERARY THEORY Jonathan Culler
LOCKE John Dunn
LOGIC Graham Priest
MACHIAVELLI Quentin Skinner
THE MARQUIS DE SADE John Phillips
MARX Peter Singer
MATHEMATICS Timothy Gowers
THE MEANING OF LIFE Terry Eagleton
MEDICAL ETHICS Tony Hope
MEDIEVAL BRITAIN John Gillingham and Ralph A. Griffiths
MEMORY Jonathan K. Foster
MODERN ART David Cottington
MODERN CHINA Rana Mitter
MODERN IRELAND Senia Pašeta
MODERN JAPAN Christopher Goto-Jones
MOLECULES Philip Ball
MORMONISM Richard Lyman Bushman
MUSIC Nicholas Cook
MYTH Robert A. Segal
NATIONALISM Steven Grosby
NELSON MANDELA Elleke Boehmer
NEOLIBERALISM Manfred Steger and Ravi Roy
THE NEW TESTAMENT Luke Timothy Johnson
THE NEW TESTAMENT AS LITERATURE Kyle Keefer
NEWTON Robert Iliffe
NIETZSCHE Michael Tanner
NINETEENTH-CENTURY BRITAIN Christopher Harvie and H. C. G. Matthew
THE NORMAN CONQUEST George Garnett
NORTHERN IRELAND Marc Mulholland
NOTHING Frank Close
NUCLEAR WEAPONS Joseph M. Siracusa
THE OLD TESTAMENT Michael D. Coogan
PARTICLE PHYSICS Frank Close
PAUL E. P. Sanders
PHILOSOPHY Edward Craig
PHILOSOPHY OF LAW Raymond Wacks
PHILOSOPHY OF SCIENCE Samir Okasha
PHOTOGRAPHY Steve Edwards
PLATO Julia Annas
POLITICAL PHILOSOPHY David Miller
POLITICS Kenneth Minogue
POSTCOLONIALISM Robert Young
POSTMODERNISM Christopher Butler
POSTSTRUCTURALISM Catherine Belsey
PREHISTORY Chris Gosden
PRESOCRATIC PHILOSOPHY Catherine Osborne
PRIVACY Raymond Wacks
PROGRESSIVISM Walter Nugent
PSYCHIATRY Tom Burns
PSYCHOLOGY Gillian Butler and Freda McManus
PURITANISM Francis J. Bremer

THE QUAKERS Pink Dandelion
QUANTUM THEORY
John Polkinghorne
RACISM Ali Rattansi
THE REFORMATION Peter Marshall
RELATIVITY Russell Stannard
RELIGION IN AMERICA Timothy Beal
THE REAGAN REVOLUTION Gil Troy
THE RENAISSANCE Jerry Brotton
RENAISSANCE ART
Geraldine A. Johnson
ROMAN BRITAIN Peter Salway
THE ROMAN EMPIRE
Christopher Kelly
ROUSSEAU Robert Wokler
RUSSELL A. C. Grayling
RUSSIAN LITERATURE Catriona Kelly
THE RUSSIAN REVOLUTION
S. A. Smith
SCHIZOPHRENIA
Chris Frith and Eve Johnstone
SCHOPENHAUER Christopher Janaway
SCIENCE AND RELIGION
Thomas Dixon
SCOTLAND Rab Houston
SEXUALITY Véronique Mottier
SHAKESPEARE Germaine Greer
SIKHISM Eleanor Nesbitt
SOCIAL AND CULTURAL
ANTHROPOLOGY
John Monaghan and Peter Just
SOCIALISM Michael Newman
SOCIOLOGY Steve Bruce
SOCRATES C. C. W. Taylor
THE SOVIET UNION
Stephen Lovell
THE SPANISH CIVIL WAR
Helen Graham
SPINOZA Roger Scruton
STATISTICS David J. Hand
STUART BRITAIN John Morrill
SUPERCONDUCTIVITY
Stephen Blundell
TERRORISM Charles Townshend
THEOLOGY David F. Ford
THOMAS AQUINAS Fergus Kerr
TRAGEDY Adrian Poole
THE TUDORS John Guy
TWENTIETH-CENTURY
BRITAIN Kenneth O. Morgan
THE UNITED NATIONS
Jussi M. Hanhimäki
THE VIKINGS
Julian Richards
WITCHCRAFT Malcolm Gaskill
WITTGENSTEIN A. C. Grayling
WORLD MUSIC Philip Bohlman
THE WORLD TRADE
ORGANIZATION
Amrita Narlikar
WRITING AND SCRIPT
Andrew Robinson

AVAILABLE SOON:

GERMAN PHILOSOPHY Andrew Bowie
DRUIDS Barry Cunliffe
FORENSIC PSYCHOLOGY
David Canter
ADVERTISING Winston Fletcher
FILM Michael Wood

For more information visit our web site
www.oup.co.uk/general/vsi/

Kathryn Kalinak

FILM MUSIC

A Very Short Introduction

OXFORD
UNIVERSITY PRESS

Oxford University Press, Inc., publishes works that further
Oxford University's objective of excellence
in research, scholarship, and education.

Oxford New York
Auckland Cape Town Dar es Salaam Hong Kong Karachi
Kuala Lumpur Madrid Melbourne Mexico City Nairobi
New Delhi Shanghai Taipei Toronto

With offices in
Argentina Austria Brazil Chile Czech Republic France Greece
Guatemala Hungary Italy Japan Poland Portugal Singapore
South Korea Switzerland Thailand Turkey Ukraine Vietnam

Published by Oxford University Press, Inc.
198 Madison Avenue, New York, NY 10016

www.oup.com

Library of Congress Cataloging-in-Publication Data
Kalinak, Kathryn Marie, 1952–
Film music : a very short introduction / Kathryn Kalinak.
p. cm. — (Very short introductions)
Includes bibliographical references and index.
ISBN 978-0-19-537087-4 (pbk.)
1. Motion picture music—History and criticism. I. Title.
ML2075.K33 2010
781.5'42—dc22
2009022731

1 3 5 7 9 8 6 4 2

Printed in Great Britain
by Ashford Colour Press Ltd., Gosport, Hants.
on acid-free paper

Contents

List of illustrations

Preface

Film music can be defined as music either directly composed or expressly chosen to accompany motion pictures. As a practice, it is as old as cinema itself—the very first projected images in many places around the globe either captured a musical performance or was accompanied by one. Even in those places where accompaniment did not initially attend motion pictures, it would soon do so. Film music has been both live and recorded, both newly composed and compiled from existing sources, both meticulously orchestrated and produced spontaneously through improvisation. It does not operate in exactly the same way across time, across cultures, and sometimes even within cultures. Across the board, however, it is characterized by its power to define meaning and to express emotion: film music guides our response to the images and connects us to them.

This very short introduction aims to provide a lucid, accessible, and engaging overview of film music from the pragmatic (what it does and how it works) to the theoretical (why it works) and from the historical (film music as a practice across time) to the personal (how film music has been practiced by the individuals who have created it). Although there will be many references to film music as music, this book is not a specialized study of music, and readers need no prior musical training.

I am guided by the need to introduce film music through a global perspective. Although the United States and Western Europe were the first places where film and music were experienced together, the story does not end there. When films first came to Japan was there musical accompaniment? What kind of music was first heard in accompaniment to films in India or Iran or Brazil? How did synchronized film scores transform the film industry in India? In Egypt? In China? How have political events around the world—World War II, the Russian Revolution, the Cultural Revolution, and the Islamic Revolution—impacted film composers and the practice of their craft?

Answering these questions and others like them has been among my highest priorities. Film music scholarship has developed over the last twenty-five years into a formidable body of knowledge on the subject, but its blind spot has been nothing less than most of the world. As this is but a very short introduction and the world is a very big place, I have had to make choices about what to include. I have tried to focus on the major film industries around the world, but even this endeavor has been limited by the lack of information about film music in some of the world's largest film industries. The choices have been difficult, and I apologize in advance for the oversights on my part. The situation is much the same with my viewing selections. At the end of the book there are suggestions for further reading and viewing. I have chosen to limit viewing selections to what is currently available on DVD, the common currency of the moment; it is dismaying to discover how many films I cannot include because they are not available in this format. The situation is especially dire when it comes to silent films with their original scores. Nevertheless, it is my hope that this very small volume will spark a very big interest in the global practice of film music.

For the sake of readability, I have followed the practice of *The Oxford History of World Cinema* with respect to foreign film titles and names. Where an English translation or transliteration of a foreign film title is available, I have used it, with the exception of films that are distinctly known by their foreign titles. Filmmakers are referred to by the names they are known by in the West. This has resulted in some inconsistencies, especially in terms of Chinese-language filmmakers: John Woo, for example, with the family name last, but Wong Kar-wai with the family name first. I apologize in advance for the many inconsistencies produced by grappling with the world's many languages through the prism of only one of them.

Chapter 1
What does film music do?

What does film music do? Since many in the audience do not even hear it, what good is it? I'd like to begin to answer these questions by looking at film music in action, by analyzing how music operates in a sequence I hope will be familiar to most readers: the torture sequence from Quentin Tarantino's *Reservoir Dogs* (1992), which features the song "Stuck in the Middle With You."

Film music, whether it is a pop song, an improvised accompaniment, or an originally composed cue, can do a variety of things. It can establish setting, specifying a particular time and place; it can fashion a mood and create atmosphere; it can call attention to elements onscreen or offscreen, thus clarifying matters of plot and narrative progression; it can reinforce or foreshadow narrative developments and contribute to the way we respond to them; it can elucidate characters' motivations and help us to know what they are thinking; it can contribute to the creation of emotions, sometimes only dimly realized in the images, both for characters to emote and for audiences to feel. Film music can unify a series of images that might seem disconnected on their own and impart a rhythm to their unfolding. While it is doing all of this, film music encourages our absorption into the film by distracting us from its technological basis—its constitution as a series of two-dimensional, larger-than-life, sometimes black-and-white, and sometimes silent, images. Of course, film music doesn't do all of these things all of the time. But music is so useful to film because it can do so much simultaneously.

A multipurpose music cue

Take the song "Stuck in the Middle With You," heard blasting from an onscreen radio accompanying the torture of a uniformed cop at the mercy of a psychotic criminal, Mr. Blonde. A bubblegum hit of the 1970s recorded by Stealers Wheel and aimed at the teen and preteen market, the song by conventional measures is no more memorable any other catchy tune of that era. But in *Reservoir Dogs* it demonstrates how music can be a controlling force in determining how we respond to a film.

One of film music's primary functions is to create mood, an important component in how an audience responds. A torture sequence would seemingly create considerable tension in an audience forced to watch it. What is so interesting about "Stuck in the Middle With You" is its power both to alter that expected mood and to distance us from the violence. The very elements that make the song sound innocuous—its chirpy melody, conventional rhythms, banal lyrics, and predictable and uncomplicated harmonies—belie the grisly nature of the sequence, dissipating the tension inherent in the situation and replacing it with an uncomfortable irony. The music is, in fact, so powerful in creating mood that when Mr. Blonde momentarily walks outside the warehouse where the torture is taking place and the song drops out, the mood is dramatically altered. Tarantino is certainly not the first nor the last director to pair brutal images with frothy music for ironic effect: Stanley Kubrick pioneered the practice in *A Clockwork Orange* (1971), where "Singin' in the Rain" accompanied a graphic murder. In fact, it has become so commonplace to accompany violence with lighthearted music that the *New York Times* titled its 1994 commentary on the practice "It's Got a Nice Beat, You Can Torture to It." The pairing of brutality with bubbly music in *Reservoir Dogs* remains amazingly effective, nonetheless.

Songs, when the audience recognizes them, can be a particularly effective way of generating a specific atmosphere. Remember that we've been told what we need to know about the song by Mr. Blonde—"Ever listen to K-Billy's Super Sounds of the 70s?"—and the deejay who introduces it as a "Dylanesque pop bubblegum favorite." Few of us might remember the 1970s, but if we do, a certain set of associations are activated: the vapidness of the "me" generation, its superficiality, its apathy. For audience members who can recall these associations, the banality of the song is heightened and the irony produced by the unsettling mixture of the trite and the terrifying is intensified. The song begins:

> Well, I don't know why I came here tonight,
> I got the feeling that something ain't right

The first stanza then moves in the next lines to the near-rhyme "chair" and "stairs," placing these everyday objects in the context of such anxiety-causing verbs as "scare" and "fall." The rhyme scheme breaks down even further as the stanza ends with the memorable lines:

> Clowns to the left of me,
> Jokers to the right, here I am,
> Stuck in the middle with you.

The lyrics—and they are heard here by both the audience and the characters—add yet another dimension. Present in the sequence is Mr. Orange, a wounded undercover police officer posing as a member of the criminal gang, incapacitated by a life-threatening wound but still alive and armed. Although present, Mr. Orange is not the focal point of the narrative, and we see him only in the background of a few shots. It is interesting how the lyrics of the song beckon us to pay attention to him. Indeed, "something ain't right" as Mr. Orange finds himself "stuck in the middle." Now the song no longer seems merely an ironic juxtaposition to the images. The lyrics have enriched our understanding of the narrative by directing our attention to a complicating factor in the scene, Mr. Orange's moral dilemma: does he blow his cover and save the cop, or sacrifice the cop for the sake of the sting operation and the apprehension of the entire gang? Tarantino has pointed out that the audience is "stuck" too: "You are stuck there, and the cinema isn't going to help you out. Every minute for that cop is a minute for you."

"Stuck in the Middle With You" guides our response by creating mood; its lyrics direct our attention to Mr. Orange while they simultaneously provide a wry commentary on our own position as spectators. But this song has much more to tell us. Film music can also provide insight into character psychology. Remember that it is Mr. Blonde himself who turns on the radio for chirpy accompaniment to his grisly torture and then begins to dance. I would argue that music renders Mr. Blonde's psychotic sadism more viscerally and thus more effectively than the dialogue. Mr. Blonde describes torturing a cop as "amusing," but it is the music that drives home his psychopathology.

Further, film music shapes our very perception. Visual representation can be vague and unspecific. Are Mr. Blonde's facial expressions, for instance, really encoding sadism, or is it perhaps insanity or maybe it's just a blank stare? Film has developed an arsenal of weapons for controlling narrative connotation including acting, dialogue cues, expressive configurations of mise-en-scène and cinematography, and specific editing patterns. Music, however, remains among the most reliable of them. It is the music, its ebullience and joyfulness, in conjunction with the grisly torture, that helps us to interpret the facial expression of Mr. Blonde as sadistic.

Film music can also create and resonate emotion between the screen and the audience. When we recognize an emotion attributed to characters or events, we become more invested in them. In a sense, the film feels more immediate, more real.

Music is one of the most powerful emotional prompts in film, encouraging us to empathize with onscreen characters. What is so interesting about this particular sequence is how music complicates emotional empathy. The song undercuts the emotions that would conventionally connect us to the tortured cop and instead promotes an emotional connection to a psychopath.

What's more, the infectious joy of the song with its visceral rhythms and catchy melody has made the sequence, well, enjoyable. Says Tarantino: "[Y]ou hear that guitar strain, you get into it, you're tapping your toe and you're enjoying Michael Madsen [Mr. Blonde] doing his dance and then, *voom*, it's too late, you're a co-conspirator." It's all guilty fun until the sequence becomes so violent that it isn't so enjoyable anymore. Music promotes our pleasure in the violence. To say that our emotions are conflicted is an understatement. Music plays a part, perhaps the primary part, in creating this conflict and then making us feel guilty for it, contributing substantially to the much vaunted "cool" psychodynamic of the film.

The role of the music supervisor

The score for *Reservoir Dogs* is different from a traditional film score where a composer creates original music. For *Reservoir Dogs,* musical selections were culled from a variety of preexisting sources, an approach known as a compilation score. It is generally the job of the music supervisor to make these selections and clear copyright for them. Usually the music supervisor works to realize the vision of the director, but some directors have taken control of the process, choosing the musical selections themselves. Tarantino is a case in point, but there are many others including Woody Allen, Wong Kar-wai, and Pedro Almodóvar. Wong Kar-wai has described the choice of music as among the first and most determining decisions he makes in preproduction. For *Chungking Express* (1994), he did not yet have a script when he described the project to his cinematographer by playing The Mamas and the Papas' "California Dreamin'," a song that plays a key role in the film. Tarantino's compilation scores are noted for their eclecticism and informed by a vast knowledge of music and film music. *Kill Bill I* and *II* (2003, 2004), for instance, contains Nancy Sinatra's cover of Sonny and Cher's "Bang Bang," songs by Isaac Hayes, Tomoyasu Hotei, Charlie Feathers, Al Hirt, Quincy Jones, Meiko Kaji, and cues from Ennio Morricone's score for *Death Rides a Horse* (1968), Bernard Herrmann's for *Twisted Nerve* (1968), and Quincy Jones's for the television series *Ironsides*. Interestingly, the job of music supervisor has opened up an economic space for women in film music. Although Elizabeth Firestone and Ann Ronell found some work in the studio era, Shirley Walker scored a number of blockbusters in the 1990s and 2000s, and Rachel Portman is thriving, female composers have found access to Hollywood film scoring limited. Women, however, now dominate the ranks of music supervisors in Hollywood.

"Stuck in the Middle With You" also helps to unify the sequence. By using a piece of music to structure the sequence, Tarantino gives it a logic and coherence that it might not have had otherwise. Certainly the music is instrumental in setting up the boundaries of the sequence. But the song's rhythms also dictate the editing, foregrounding the music. The song gives the sequence its lyricism, if that's the right word for such a sequence, its infectious energy that draws us into it, absorbing us into filmic spectacle.

Film music's many functions

Film music shapes meaning on a number of levels. Audiences will respond to film music with varying degrees of awareness, but at least some of the operation of film music takes place on a less than fully conscious plane. I discuss this particular aspect of film music in much greater detail in chapter 3, but here I would point out that when film music operates under the radar of consciousness, it has intensified power to affect us. Film music can cause us to engage with meanings and pull us toward responses without our knowing it, such as getting us to enjoy a scene of torture.

There is one facet of "Stuck in the Middle With You" that the majority of the audience may not have apprehended on a fully conscious level. While most of the audience will be aware of the presence of the song, and many will register that this is a song from the 1970s and pay attention to its lyrics, and some may be cognizant of the irony and emotional turmoil produced by the song, few will realize that the volume of music has been manipulated. "Stuck in the Middle With You" could not possibly conform to the way it is seen to be generated on screen. Mr. Blonde turns on the radio at which point the song is introduced. Initially, it sounds as if "Stuck in the Middle With You" is coming over the airwaves in monophonic sound, preceded by crackling transmission noises consistent with the dated radio and its limited sound capacity. However, on the cut to the close-up of the anguished cop, quickly followed by the long shot of Mr. Blonde beginning to dance, the volume on the song has been turned up, way up, and the quality of the sound improves from the thin, monophonic sound of the radio to a fully stereophonic rendition. The music has been manipulated to intensify its joyfulness, and that we are not conscious of this manipulation increases our enjoyment. The manipulation of volume makes it easier to deal with Mr. Blonde and thus sets us up for the complicated responses we have to the sequence.

"Stuck in the Middle With You" has performed a variety of functions here. It has created mood, helped to establish atmosphere, aided in characterization, helped to shape the narrative, fashioned a complicated emotional response for the audience, especially in terms of the representation of violence, unified the sequence, given it its rhythm, and absorbed the audience into the spectacle of the film. And it has forced us to identify with a sadistic criminal.

These observations about the function of music in narrative film are not unique to *Reservoir Dogs*. I've chosen this example because it demonstrates so many of the key properties of film music. This is not to say that film music is a kind of universal language. Music in Hollywood film operates quite differently from the way it does in Hindi cinema, which uses music differently than Bengali cinema does, which uses music again differently from the way it is used in Brazilian cinema. Specific national and cultural traditions have created distinct practices of film music throughout the world, and those specific histories have evolved across time, as we shall see. Even so, music has an expressive power that crosses many borders, and film traditions throughout the world have harnessed music's expressive power to shape perception of the film and to reverberate emotion between the spectator and the screen.

Chapter 2
How does film music work?

Film music lies at the intersection of film and music, an obvious enough observation, but probing this intersection fully is crucial to understanding how film music operates. Film music inherits part of its ability to make meaning from its constitution as a musical practice and another part from its constitution as a cinematic practice. Although it is often recorded or performed, marketed, and heard purely as music, film music is nevertheless defined by its function within a cinematic field of reference. Thus, music in film is always something of a hybrid. In this chapter I introduce some of the basic ways in which film music can be meaningful, first in terms of its constitution as music, and second in terms of its function as a component of filmic narrative.

Film music as a musical practice

This book is not intended as a specialized study of music, and it requires no musical training on the part of its readers. But film music is, after all, music, and like any meaning system, it depends upon certain forms and structures, and the patterns of meaning contained in them, to make it intelligible. Just as we learn to read a film, that is, to connect specific meanings to the various techniques at the filmmaker's disposal (such as an editing dissolve, which tells us that time has passed), so, too, we can learn to read music, that is, to identify the basic building blocks of music (such as tonality, melody, harmony, rhythm, tempo, dynamics, timbre, instrumentation, and form) at the disposal of the composer, and connect specific meanings to them. If this process seems more intimidating for music than for film, it may be that our more extended acquaintance with visual media has made reading images seem easier. But remember that we had to learn to read films, too.

Although music is universal (all human cultures that have left records appear to have produced it), music is by no means a universal language shared among all people across time. Throughout human history, music has been constituted in a myriad of ways. The music of the Western world, as it coalesced around a set of principles in the Early Modern Period, is but one of them. It provides a useful entry point into understanding film music, however, for a variety of reasons. Western music exerted a powerful influence globally in the late nineteenth and early twentieth centuries at the very moment when film music was developing; thus it played a large part in the history of musical accompaniment around the world. And it is the musical system with which most English-speaking readers will be familiar. As I present this material, however, I will try to include examples from non-Western musics, which I hope will function as a contrapuntal voice as well as a reminder that Western music is only one kind of music among many worldwide.

The basic building blocks of Western music hinge upon *tonality*, a structure for organizing musical sounds into music. Tonality may be defined as a musical system revolving around a single tone or note, which functions as a center of gravity: it is a focal point around which the rest of the notes are organized and which serves as the place where a piece of music begins and ends. Other systems of music employ tonality. Classical Indian music and many kinds of Middle Eastern music, for example, depend upon a single tone droned throughout an entire piece to provide a stable tonal base. Western music works in a different way, producing tension and release as the music moves alternatively away from and toward a tonal center. Tonality can be subdivided in a number of ways, but one important division is the one between major and minor tonalities, two organizing modes that can carry specific associations and can impart very distinct inflections. While there is nothing inherently happy or sad about music composed in a major or minor mode, associations of happiness and brightness are often attached to the major mode while associations of melancholy and ominousness are attached to the minor.

A distinguishing characteristic of tonal music, since about the middle of the eighteenth century, is the privileging of *melody*, a series of notes played in a memorable and recognizable order. Melody provides an access point into music, a hook on which to hang listeners' attention. Western music is not alone in utilizing melody. Classical Indian music, for instance, is built on melodies that have coalesced over centuries into a body of recognizable and commonly shared rāgas, each with a unique melodic pattern and a fixed association such as tranquility, heroism, power, or pathos. Thus film composers in India, both in the traditional background score and in film songs, can easily access powerful musical structures for creating mood and atmosphere through the use of rāgas.

Film composers around the globe have engaged melody. A. R. Rahman, the Indian composer of the songs and score for *Slumdog Millionaire* (2008), credits melody with "a very important role in my sensibility in music." Melody, however, has been a hallmark of Hollywood scoring. John Barry explains, "I love working with melody. I think if you can capture something in the simplest possible way, which is what melody is, then you're halfway there." Claims Randy Newman: "I believe in melody. Maybe there are places where you don't want it, but I don't know where they'd be." Melody has often taken the form of a *leitmotif*, an identifiable and recurring musical pattern. A leitmotif can consist of any kind of musical material—a distinctive rhythm, for instance—but

Hollywood composers have tended to construct leitmotifs through melody, either as short as a motif of a few notes or as extended as a theme. Leitmotifs can be developed and varied throughout the score (or repeated verbatim), reinforcing associations and becoming more and more powerful as a film progresses. The final reiteration of a leitmotif—especially when it coincides with the end of a film—can have an enormous emotional impact. Still, not all Hollywood composers privilege melody—just try humming the shower sequence from Bernard Herrmann's score for *Psycho* (1960)—but melody is nonetheless a powerful tool for shaping a score.

Harmony has to do with the coordination of notes playing simultaneously. In Western tonal music, harmony privileges certain combinations of notes, or chords, over others, creating stress points built upon dissonance and resolutions that dissipate dissonance. The farther harmony moves from the tonal center, the more associations of disorder and instability will be activated; the closer to the tonal center, the more associations of order and stability. Harmony is often less immediately recognizable than melody, but its effects are powerful and discernible even by those without the language to describe them. Interestingly, harmony is not a requirement of music, and many musical practices throughout history and around the globe are not harmonic in the way that Western tonal music is. Musical systems that depend upon improvisation, such as Indian and Middle Eastern, lack a focus on harmony in the Western sense, and early music from many places around the globe, including the West, do not depend upon it. And the set of seven tones or notes that comprise Western music's harmonic system represents only one such organizational structure. The pentatonic scale, used in many Asian and Native American musics, uses five tones. Western music harnesses the ability of tonal harmony to powerfully and predictably create and dissipate tension.

Rhythm refers to the organization of music through time; its basic unit is the beat, a discernible pulse that marks out the passage of time. Western music is characterized by a high degree of regularity in terms of rhythm, and deviations from established patterns can be very potent. Many music systems throughout the world depend upon rhythms, although they may operate differently than in Western music. In Indian music, musical rhythms have coalesced into established patterns far more complicated than Western rhythms. In Western music, a rhythm can be established in as few as three or four beats. One traditional Indian rhythmic pattern comprises 108 separate beats before it repeats. Middle Eastern song practice, on the other hand, often does not depend upon regular rhythms but on flexible rhythms that can adjust to the lyrics. In Western tonal music, rhythm is much more predictable, operating as a sonic grid against which the composer writes.

Timbre refers to the quality of sound that distinguishes one instrument or voice from another. To hear timbre in action, we might think of the difference in Western music between art music and popular music traditions. Art music aims to produce a fairly standard timbre within a vocal range or class of instruments (which can make it difficult to distinguish one operatic soprano from another). Popular music, however, aims in the opposite direction, to distinguish one voice from another, one way of playing an instrument from another. Establishing a unique timbre is one way of doing so, and most listeners can probably tell the difference between Mariah Carey and P!nk. Timbre is a powerful worldwide musical property. It is of great importance to Japanese music, for instance, where singers and instrumentalists are trained to create a multiplicity of different timbres with the same instrument or voice. Traditional *Gidayu-bushi* singers can even customize the timbre of their voices to establish gender and age. In certain African musical traditions, the timbre of a voice is individuated by extramusical properties that many other vocal traditions attempt to minimize, such as the sound of breathing. Instrumentation can be thought of as the art of selecting different timbres, choosing one instrument or voice over another to create specific effects, using violins instead of horns, for example, or a bass voice over a tenor voice.

Listening for all of these musical properties while you watch a film may seem like a very tall order—and I haven't even included all of the musical tools at the disposal of the composer (tempo, dynamics, and musical form are obvious omissions). One of the best and easiest ways to hear these properties is through musical conventions that harness musical affects to specific meanings through the power of association. Musical conventions become ingrained in a culture and function as a kind of musical collective unconscious, affecting listeners whether or not they are consciously aware of such conventions. Think of musical conventions as a cultural shorthand that does not have to be consciously recognized by listeners to produce predictable responses. For obvious reasons, film composers depend upon musical conventions to guide and control audience response, but composers can also deliberately contradict these conventions for dramatic effect. Musical conventions do not function universally. They change across history and are culturally determined so that what works at one point in time and in one place on the globe may not in another. In Hollywood, the brass instruments have conventionally connoted heroism, but in Hindi film, brasses often signify villainy. Still, musical conventions can produce predictable audience reactions and are frequently exploited to direct an audience's emotional and psychological trajectory through a film by composers working both within Western music and outside of it.

For example, in Disney's animated feature *Beauty and the Beast* (1991), Alan Menken and Howard Ashman created the song "Beauty and the Beast," which functions as a love theme for Belle and the Beast. The song is based on well-established conventions for romantic passion: a major key, stable harmonies, a prominent use of violins (commonly thought of as the most expressive instrument in the orchestra and thus linked to passion), and a memorable melody with upward leaps in the melodic pattern. These conventions are so powerful that they connote romance whether or not an audience consciously recognizes their use. Of course in this instance lyrics emphasize these musical conventions: "Tale as old as time, song as old as rhyme." But even without the lyrics, the song has tapped into musical conventions for romance that are among the most identifiable (and some might add shopworn) strategies in Hollywood film scoring.

Musical conventions can help to create a variety of different moods and emotions. One of the most famous music cues is the one Bernard Herrmann composed for the shower sequence in *Psycho*. Herrmann exploited a number of musical conventions for invoking terror: the absence of melody, unpredictable rhythms, strident and dissonant harmonies, violins at the very top and basses at the very bottom of their ranges played with techniques that inhibit lyricism. Interestingly, Herrmann's shower cue has become such an iconic musical creation of terror that its distinctive shrieking violins have now become a convention for terror itself, evoked in countless horror films, parodies of horror films, television shows, and perhaps the real horror, television commercials.

Contemporary film composers in Hollywood have begun to tap into conventions of world music to guide and shape audience response. For Mira Nair's *Monsoon Wedding* (2001), Mychael Danna created a "Main Title" sequence based on a traditional Indian *baraat*, the wedding processional for the groom. Although there was a great deal of improvisation in the recording of this cue, it is based on a traditional Indian rāga with associations of joy and harmony. As with "Beauty and the Beast," it is not necessary for audiences to be consciously aware of the convention, in this case the identity of the *Rāga Kalyan*, for the music to transmit joy. Of course, Indian audiences who recognize the cultural reference will have a deeper experience of the music than audiences who do not, and thus Danna's choice becomes a particularly compelling one, from a multicultural perspective, for a film about India aimed at a global audience.

A film composer can even violate established musical conventions to create intriguing and disturbing effects. Ennio Morricone in *The Good, the Bad, and the Ugly* (1966) used minor keys for many of the fast-paced and thrilling action sequences, and major keys for many of the somber and melancholic sequences. Herrmann's cue for *Psycho* is a veritable blueprint for musical terror. At the same time that he invoked conventions for horror, however, Herrmann ignored the most typical convention for creating suspense—*tremolo*, or rapidly vibrating strings—and deliberately undercut another convention by using violins not for romance but for murder. In fact, the *Psycho* score is composed exclusively for strings, instruments more conventionally associated with romance.

Film music as a cinematic practice

Our experience of film music is shaped by its constitution as music. But film music does not operate in a vacuum; it functions as part of a larger system of meaning. Film itself is a narrative form. Although there are certainly films that are nonnarrative in their construction, film developed into an art form to tell stories. Music is part of this process, a key part of this process.

Music's function in film preoccupied the earliest critics and scholars of film music. In the 1930s, the first wave of film music criticism began to be published, positing that sound was subordinate to the image. Film music, those writers argued, related to the image either through parallelism—reinforcing the image's content—or through counterpoint—contradicting the image's content. This model was influenced, no doubt, by the famous "Statement on Sound Film," signed by Soviet filmmakers Sergei Eisenstein, Vsevolod Pudovkin, and Gregori Alexandrov in 1928, which categorized film sound according to whether it paralleled or counterpointed the image. Within a decade, the influential critic Theodor Adorno and composer Hanns Eisler in their groundbreaking *Composing for the Films* pointed out, "A photographed kiss cannot actually be synchronized with an eight-bar phrase." Adorno and Eisler argued that visual imagery and music are very different forms of expression, and they do not operate, in any sense, in ways that could accurately be described as parallel or contrapuntal.

Further, positing that music either parallels or counterpoints what is already "there" assumes that the image is autonomous and encodes meaning unproblematically. Even today some film music criticism continues to employ terminology that assumes the image is the bearer of meaning and that music functions to modify that meaning in some way, heightening, reinforcing, or undercutting what is "in" the image. Because visual images are representational, that is, because on the surface at least, they make direct reference to what they represent, it is easy to assume that visual images have immediate, obvious, and stable meaning. This is not always (or perhaps ever) the case. Visual images can be amorphous and ambiguous, and even the surface of an image can be open to multiple interpretations. It is problematic to assume that meaning is unproblematically "there" in the image.

There are a number of other problems with the parallel/counterpoint model as well. How can we account for film music that neither parallels nor counterpoints the image? I would find it difficult to describe "Stuck in the Middle With You" in *Reservoir Dogs* as either paralleling or counterpointing the images. The use of that song is much more complex than either of those two options can account for (see chap. 1). How can we explain those moments when the music is foregrounded and the images respond to the music, as when Mr. Blonde starts dancing to "Stuck in the Middle With You," and the editing and camerawork are driven by song's structure?

Film is a narrative medium, an art form that delivers stories. The soundtrack and the visual track always operate within this larger field of reference. Contemporary film music scholars have shaped a different model for film music's operation in which music is seen as an interdependent and complementary element of a film's narrative system. Music shares power to create meaning with a number of elements that come together to tell a story, among them mise-en-scène, cinematography, acting, editing, dialogue, and sound. When we hear tremolo strings, it is not a simple case of music reinforcing the suspense that is already "there" in the image. Instead, tremolo strings are a component of the process by which suspense is generated. The basic elements of film work together in narrative film in a "*combinatoire* of expression," Claudia Gorbman's evocative phrase.

Music can be a crucial element in this process. When we hear "Stuck in the Middle With You" in *Reservoir Dogs*, the song is not reinforcing an emotional exhilaration produced by the images. Rather it is the key component in the process by which the audience experiences a visceral thrill, a process that includes the editing, which foregrounds the music, the dialogue that sets it up, and the characterization of Mr. Blonde as psychotic. Would the torture of the cop at the hands of a psychotic killer, however, be emotionally exhilarating, on any level, were it not for the music?

Let's delve a bit more deeply into film music's function in relation to narrative. Roland Barthes's insights about the function of photographic captions offer fruitful insight here. Captions control and limit the perception of photographs, a process Barthes called *ancrage* (anchoring). Film music works in the same way, reinforcing one meaning out of many possible meanings, anchoring the image to specificity. It is as if the music "throws a net around the floating visual signifier" in Gorbman's words. And that is what Noel Carroll means when he describes film music's function as "modifying." Just as adjectives and adverbs pin down the meaning of the nouns and verbs they are attached to, film music pins down the image track. Film music polices the ways in which the audience perceives narrative and does so in a complex relationship with other elements of a film's narrative system.

Film music always works in a network of mutual implication. In the same way that music can anchor the image in specificity, the image can impart explicitness to the music by giving it referentiality, grounding the general expressiveness of the music in a specificity it might not otherwise have had. And music's function in film is always bounded by the limits of credibility itself. Imagine hearing the cue from the shower sequence of *Psycho* as Belle and the Beast dance around the ballroom in *Beauty and the Beast*. Or the song "Beauty and the Beast" as accompaniment to the grisly shower murder in *Psycho*. The farther music drifts away from mutual dependency with the rest of the elements in a narrative system, the more potential there is for disruption—and for just not making sense.

Film music anchors the image in another way as well: it positions the audience to receive the narrative in the way intended by the filmmakers.

Music resonates emotion between the audience and the screen. Narrative films have developed a number of practices to assist expressive acting in portraying emotion such as the close-up, diffuse lighting and focus, aesthetically pleasing mise-en-scène, and dialogue delivered with heightened vocal intensity. Music is the most reliable of them, harnessing the power of musical conventions to provide an audible definition of the emotion represented in the film. Elmer Bernstein puts it this way: "Music can tell the story in purely emotional terms and the film by itself cannot."

Film music does more than define emotion however—it generates it. Samuel Chell compares music in classical Hollywood film to a television laugh track, which not only tells the audience that the show is funny but prompts the audience to laugh at it. The pop song heard under a love scene both delineates the emotion that the onscreen characters feel and prompts the audience to identify with and share that emotion. By resonating emotion between the audience and the screen, film music engages audiences in processes of identification, which bind them into the film.

The first time we hear the song "Beauty and the Beast," it precedes any declaration of love on the part of the couple. Belle and the Beast find themselves "alone" together in the ballroom of the Beast's enchanted castle. Previously Belle has spurned the Beast's attentions, but he has just saved her life, and their icy relationship has thawed. The enchanted dinnerware and household items are doing everything they can to encourage an attachment. But no word of love is spoken. Are they or are they not falling in love? A number of cinematic elements are at work here to encourage the audience to believe that they are. First, there's the "acting" (the look on Belle's face, the exchange of looks between the Beast and the servants) and the spectacular animation focusing on them as a couple ("camerawork," editing, and supposedly the first use of computer-generated imagery in the Disney canon). Then there are extratextual factors that come into play: the well-known fairy tale on which the film is based and the audience's knowledge of other Disney animated films that end with the uniting of the couple. But the music is the crucial part of the process. The rhapsodic music exploiting conventions for passion such as violins and an upward trajectory in the melodic line, in combination with a major key, stable harmonics, and the lyrics, which voice the age-old story of romance, anchors the image to a particular meaning—that they are falling in love—while simultaneously encouraging us to participate in the couple's emotional register.

Music functions as part of an interdependent and complicated process of narrative construction in film by controlling connotation and positioning the audience to respond. This model, however, leaves some questions unanswered. Film music certainly has a narrative function, but does it always have a narrative function? Does film music ever function nonnarratively? According to Jerrold Levinson, it does indeed. While most film music can be defined by its function in relation to narrative, some film music cannot. Levinson's litmus test: if the music were deleted, would the narrative content be altered in any way? If the answer is yes, then music is functioning as an element in the narrative process.

Not all film music functions in this way according to Levinson. Some does not contribute to the construction of the narrative but functions instead as an "additive," music that adds to the film but not to the narrative. An example would be music that lends coherence or unity to a film, such as music that bridges a sequence to smooth over gaps in time. Music here functions not as an element in the construction of the narrative but as an element in the construction of the film. For Levinson, music can even function both narratively and nonnarratively at the same time. While contemporary theorists agree that film music is part of a complex narrative process in film, they continue to debate a number of issues including whether all of film music's functions are narrative.

To sum up: film music is capable of powerful effects, and those effects are the product of a unique amalgamation between two art forms. Again, film music lies at the intersection of music and film, and to understand fully how it operates we must consider both its constitution as a musical practice and its function within a cinematic practice. Music fulfills a number of important functions as an element in a film's narrative system. And it depends upon the properties of music to do so.

Chapter 3
Why does film music work?

Why does film music have such power over us? What are the sources of its pleasures? And why should music have come to accompany film at all? To answer such intriguing questions, we are going to need *theory*, a body of thought devoted to analyzing the deep and complex issues that underlie the framework of a discipline. Theory delves beneath the surface to get at what is neither obvious nor easily answered. Theory is always open to debate: it can be controversial and contradictory, obfuscating and illuminating, sometimes all at once. But without theory we risk becoming locked into unexamined patterns of thinking, and we cannot come to terms with those fundamental questions posed above.

A lively theoretical discourse has grown up around the sources of film's powers and pleasures, and the ways in which they are tied to the presence of music in film. Incorporating the insights of structural linguistics, psychoanalysis, Marxism, cultural studies, and cognitive theory, theorists of film music have investigated why music is such a potent force in film (indeed why music is a force in films at all) and what we get out of listening to it. In this chapter I'll introduce some important theories of film music and the theorists who have espoused them. Of course, theory has already informed this book, and if you have gotten this far, you have already been introduced to some theoretically informed observations in chapter 1 and some core theoretical issues in chapter 2. But this chapter puts theory on the front burner, so to speak, because to answer complex questions, we need theory. As I hope to show, theory is not only an indispensable component in examining the fundamental questions of film music, it also constitutes a fascinating aspect of the discipline in its own right.

But before we move into film theory, a brief detour into film history would be helpful. Why did music come to accompany moving images at all? Film exerted a gravitational pull toward music from the very beginning, both in the countries where film originated and in the countries where it arrived (see chap. 4). The standard explanation for the amalgamation of image and music is functional: music compensated for the lack of sound in silent film, and it covered the noise produced both by the projector and by audiences unschooled in cinema etiquette. Music was readily available in the early homes of cinema, the cafes, vaudeville theaters, music halls, carnivals, and traveling exhibitions where musicians would play for the moving images on the program as they would for live performances. But noisy projectors and audiences were soon quieted, motion pictures moved into their own screening spaces, and it wasn't long before synchronized sound became the norm. Yet musical accompaniment persisted in film long after its initial utility had faded. As chapter 3 has shown, music serves many functions in film. But understanding how film music works is not the same thing as understanding why it works. We need to understand what sustained music as a practice throughout film history. What made it indispensable?

It is interesting how early scholars turned toward theory to answer this question. In 1936 Kurt London posited that it was music's ability to provide unity through regular, predictable, and audible rhythms that made it indispensable to film, a medium comprised of individual shots, irregular in length, structure, and content. In the mid-twentieth century, Jean Mitry similarly identified music's ultimate utility to film as its power to unify, a function of its construction as an art form constituted by time. Mitry identified music's "fundamental rhythmic structure" as that which imparts to film "what it lacks: the notion of temporality." Through rhythm, music's ordered articulation of time is transferred to film itself. Music thus provides continuity for a medium that is, by its nature, marked by discontinuity.

The contemporary theorist Michel Chion argues that film needs music because it makes images pliable. Music allows film "to wander at will through time and space," inducing the audience to accept the cinematic manipulation of time and space through editing. But if Chion echoes earlier theories for the presence of music in film, he also opens up new avenues to explore. For Chion, music serves a unifying function not because it is constituted through time but because it is independent of the constraints of time. Thus music provides a "unifying sound bath" that, by overflowing the limits of the individual shots, can connect separate images in a film to each other, "homogenizing" them. Before Chion, Claudia Gorbman posited that with the onset of sound cinema, the sound track reconstructed time into a "relentless linearity" with music being "the one sound element capable of freeing up that temporal representation." This explains why music is called upon to attend film's most fractious moments in terms of time—flashbacks, montages, and slow-motion sequences—that threaten the unity of the film.

The powers of film music

Theory has also addressed more primal questions regarding the sources of film music's powers and pleasures. An investigation of these sources has led theorists in two directions: outward toward culture where film music is produced, and inward toward consciousness where film music is perceived.

The idea that music is a product of culture owes much of its existence to the Frankfurt School, a body of critical thought generated in and around Frankfurt, Germany, in the 1920s. Marxist critics associated with the Frankfurt School, especially Theodor Adorno and other German intellectuals such as Bertold Brecht and Ernst Bloch, examined the forces of economics, politics, and culture that shaped the production of art under capitalism. Attacking cherished notions of art's autonomous function, the unique creativity of the artist, and the ability of the individual to resist cultural contexts, the Frankfurt School asserted that art is part of a complex and vast apparatus that largely reinforces the dominant ideological values of capitalism.

Music, like any art form, is a social discourse, structured by a set of social relations between artist and perceiver. For Adorno, music has a unique position among the arts. Because it seems more direct and less mediated by culture, music actually has the most power to serve a political function under capitalism: to pacify dangerous, anarchic impulses by lulling listeners into an acceptance of the status quo, distracting them from the alienating effects of life under capitalism.

Adorno, in collaboration with composer Hanns Eisler, extended this argument to film music in their groundbreaking text, *Composing for the Films*. Music binds the spectator into the film and masks the film's material constitution as a technological product. Film music for Adorno and Eisler is "a cement, which holds together elements that otherwise would oppose each other unrelated—the mechanical product and the spectators." Film music's adhesion stems from its exceptional ability to create and resonate emotion between the screen and the spectator. In so doing, film music distracts spectators from film's materiality. Thus film music fulfills a potent ideological function: to promote an audience's absorption into the film and thus position that audience to accept, uncritically, the cultural values circulating through a film. It is not without significance that Adorno and Eisler refer to film music as a drug. That art serves a political function was a radical notion in postwar America. Adorno's authorship of *Composing for the Films* was suppressed in English-language editions, and Eisler, who had found work composing film scores in Hollywood, was summoned before the House Un-American Activities Committee and forced to leave the United States. That art is inextricably tied to politics seems painfully obvious in Eisler's case.

Other theorists following in the wake of the Frankfurt School have explored music's subversive power. Jacques Attali, for example, in *Noise: The Political Economy of Music,* argues that music is never innocent. He agrees with Adorno that it is a tool of social coercion, reflecting and sustaining the structure of the political order. However, Attali also believes in the subversive power of music and in the possibility of radical social change through noise, the liberation of music's suppressed anarchic power.

The ideological analysis of film music has been taken up by many film scholars. In Claudia Gorbman's pioneering text, *Unheard Melodies*: *Narrative Film Music*, Gorbman opens up Adorno and Eisler's insights by comparing film music to easy-listening music. The similarities are illuminating. Both operate as part of a larger field of reference, whether the shopping mall, the dentist's office, or narrative film; both are regulated by a larger context, which determines its presence or absence, the interruption of a mall's background music to make announcements, or the decreased volume of the film score under dialogue; neither draws attention to itself nor demands the listener's full attention; and both drive away unpleasantness, whether it be the drilling in the dentist's office or the technological basis of cinema. Music encourages us to consume the products of culture and makes consumption easy, whether the product is material, such as the goods on display at the mall, or immaterial, such as film images. Ultimately, Gorbman theorizes, film music lulls "the spectator into becoming an *untroublesome* (less critical, less wary) *viewing subject*." Film music makes us more likely to brush away doubts about what the film might be promoting, to suspend our disbelief in the two-dimensional, larger-than-life images posing as reality, and ultimately to accept, uncritically, a series of images and the cultural values they encode.

Similarly intrigued by music's ideological function in film, Caryl Flinn, in *Strains of Utopia: Gender, Nostalgia, and Hollywood Film Music*, theorizes that one of the most potent discourses attached to music is a "utopian" discourse: music's ability to offer "an impression of perfection and integrity in an otherwise imperfect and unintegrated world." Music offers listeners a "fullness of experience . . . an ability to return . . . to better, allegedly more 'perfect' times and memories." Film scores transport listeners from the technological and fragmented experience of a postindustrial capitalism and its mechanically reproduced art forms to an idealized past of wholeness. According to this argument, film music always carries with it traces of plenitude, wrapping film content in a kind of nostalgia and making us desire what the film offers. In the process we become less critical of a film's values and value judgments.

Theory can seem exceedingly abstract, but its application can have profound consequences for our understanding of film. The manner in which cultural ideology manifests itself through music is neither direct, because much of its operation takes place on less than a conscious plane, nor is it immediately obvious; it is complex, sometimes contradictory, and elusive. The results of that process, however, are clearly audible to any listener. When in a 1940s or 1950s Hollywood film you hear a bluesy saxophone in accompaniment to a woman on screen, what do you assume about her sexuality? What difference would it make to hear a lush romantic cue featuring a sweet violin instead? Hollywood composers depended upon a set of musical conventions to represent female sexuality. These clichéd conventions (saxophones and bluesy performance practices for women whose sexuality operated outside social norms, violins in upward trajectories for virtuous girlfriends, wives, and especially mothers) encoded a set of responses and value judgments consistent with dominant cultural values about female sexuality. Take a listen to the score for *Bladerunner* (1982) and its iconic use of the saxophone to judge for yourself how far film music has come—or not—with regard to the treatment of female characters.

The ideological function of film music has been an especially rich site of investigation for contemporary film music scholars who have examined how concepts such as history, gender, sexuality, race, class, and ethnicity are encoded in a film's score. Some recent examples of the diverse body of scholarship emerging in this area—and this is a very short list limited to book-length monographs—would have to include Krin Gabbard's analyses of the ways that jazz encodes cultural ideologies about race and sexuality; Anahid Kassabian's study of the impact of song choice in the representation of gender in contemporary Hollywood film; Caryl Flinn's study of music and the relationship between history, culture, and ideology in New German film; and my own study of the ideological function of song in the westerns of John Ford.

The pleasures of film music

Film music is produced through culture, but it is perceived by individuals. A significant amount of film music is perceived consciously: we wouldn't come out of a film remembering its music or be induced to buy a soundtrack recording otherwise. But if we are to analyze fully film music's power and understand the pleasures it offers us, we need to address how film music works in another register—in the unconscious. Watching film is enjoyable. It has a unique hold over us, an ability to make us forget where we are or who we are when we are engrossed in watching it. Psychoanalysis, a theory of the mind that seeks to understand the operation of the unconscious, can help us grasp why this hypnotic fascination is so pleasurable and specifically what part music plays in this fascination.

Beginning in the 1970s and 1980s, French and North American theorists turned to psychoanalysis to bring music into focus. Music plays a key role in human psychic development. From our earliest moments inside the womb, we experience the elements of music: the rhythmic patterns of our mother's heartbeat, breathing, and pulse as well as the pitch and dynamics of her voice. In fact, the womb is often described in psychoanalysis in acoustic terms as a "sonorous envelope of the self," in the words of Didier Anzieu, the "sonorous space" of Gerard Blanchard, or "the murmuring house" of Guy Rosolato. We know, for instance, that a newborn can already recognize its mother's voice. After birth, the infant continues in a bath of aural stimulation, including and especially the mother's voice, which, again, is experienced as music. (Think of the ways in which language itself incorporates musical elements such as rhythm, pitch, dynamics, and intonation and the musical way we talk to babies.) Psychoanalysis posits the pleasure of music as stemming from both our pre-birth experience as well as our earliest, pre-linguistic existence. Music allows us to experience what we are forced to repress in our adult lives: longings for a return to the original state of plentitude and fusion with the mother, a fusion we experienced as music. Rosolato argues that Western harmony, with its patterns of divergence and unity, can be understood psychoanalytically as the "dramatization of these separated and reunited bodies" of mother and child. But it is not only Western music that can claim a connection between its music and elemental psychic processes. The famed *taiko* drummer Daihaichi Oguchi explained the lure of the taiko drum in similar terms: "Your heart is a taiko. All people listen to a taiko rhythm '*dontsuku-dontsuku*' in their mother's womb."

Psychoanalysis helps to account for music's centrality in human experience. Music stimulates us to regress back to that complete sense of satisfaction and pleasure that the union with the mother represents. When we watch films and hear film music, something similar happens. A number of factors, the comfortable seats, the darkened auditorium, the hypnotic effect of the bright images on the screen, and the music come together to encourage us to regress back to a psychic state of profound plenitude and satisfaction. This is what gives film music such a powerful hold over us and at least partially explains why it is in film at all. Film music short-circuits consciousness, as Gorbman points out, "bypassing the usual censors of the preconscious," facilitating the hypnotic power of film and encouraging us to regress to a place of complete psychic satisfaction. No wonder we love going to the movies!

Psychoanalytically informed theories of film music have come under fire from cognitive theorists who argue that psychoanalysis ignores the conscious work performed by audiences as they experience a film. Pointing to the successful soundtrack recording industry, the popularity of songs conceived for films, and the millions of film music fans around the world, among other reasons, cognitivists posit that we interpret music in the same way that we do any other cinematic element: by processing the information it presents us. For example, Ben Winters argues that it is our active engagement with musical conventions that allows us to simulate the emotions experienced by on-screen characters and share in their response, a process he describes as "far from subliminal." Jeff Smith has written the most sustained cognitivist critique of psychoanalytic film music theory by posing a series of difficult questions, among them: how does psychoanalysis account for the intermittence of film music? Since film music, in sound film at least, is not a continuous but a fragmentary phenomenon, how are the unconscious processes it activates sustained when it is absent? What is the relationship between the unconscious and conscious perception of film music? How much or what part of music is "unheard"? Cognitive film theorists argue that a psychoanalytic theory of film music is not yet fully realized and needs to take into account a number of unresolved issues. But if we are looking for the sources of our fascination with film music and our pleasures in listening to it, we should not dismiss the relationship between music and the unconscious. Although we do not access it consciously, this facet of music cannot be discounted in a theory of what pleases and engages us when we listen to film music.

So where has this journey into theory taken us? It has offered some thought-provoking ideas about the sources of music's powers and pleasures. But more than that, this chapter hopefully prompts deeper and more far-reaching reflections on both the nature of power, how it circulates through culture and is manifested through its art forms, and the power of the unconscious, which underlies all of human activity.

Chapter 4
A history of film music I: 1895–1927

The history of film music, like the history of film itself, is an unfinished story and always will be. Much of the earliest evidence has been lost; overgeneralizations and misinformation abound; and much of what we know of this history has been focused on the United States and Western Europe. This much is clear: music was present at the dawn of film and found its way into this new medium as it journeyed around the globe.

Music and the origins of motion pictures

"The idea occurred to me that it was possible to devise an instrument which should do for the eye what the phonograph does for the ear," Thomas Edison famously wrote. But it is his description of what he imagined that instrument could do that underscores the primacy of music in Edison's enterprise. "Thus if one wished to hear or see a concert or the opera, it would only be necessary to sit down at home, look upon a screen and see the performance reproduced exactly...and at the same time the voices of the players and singers [and] the music of the orchestra." While Edison never realized his visionary concept of audio-visual home entertainment, music was to prove central to the history of motion pictures.

One early effort at synchronized sound at the Edison laboratories has survived in an experimental film made around 1894 by

W. K. L. Dickson, head of Edison's motion picture division. Two male employees dance to music from Robert Planquette's 1877 light opera *The Chimes of Normandy*, played by Dickson himself on the violin into the phonograph horn visible in the frame. It is the only known surviving example of audio-visual synchronization at Edison. Dickson's performance is often cited as the first example of musical accompaniment, but that description does not do justice to the driving force of music here. In some sense, it is the images that accompany the music. And, while Dickson's film may well have been a step toward Edison's dream of opera in the home, its music could well point in another direction, the centrality of popular music in early film accompaniment. "Song of the Cabin Boy," the piece Dickson played, may be derived from a "high art" source, but it was repackaged as a popular song and marketed for mass consumption by the time Dickson played it, an early example of crossover music.

By this time, however, Edison had already shifted focus to the more commercially viable Kinetoscope, a peep-show device debuting publicly in 1894, which presented silent moving images to a single spectator. Although the synchronization of image and sound had stalled, the quest for musical accompaniment had not. Beginning in 1895, the Kinetophone, a modified Kinetoscope outfitted with a phonograph and ear tubes, presented preexisting Edison films—largely musical performances of one sort or another—accompanied by specifically chosen phonograph recordings from the Edison catalogue. These presentations were not synchronized; rather the music was chosen to loosely fit the images. What evidence there is (and it is scant) suggests that popular dance tunes and marches were used in these match-ups: "La Paloma" for *Carmencita*; an Irish jig for *Lucy Murray* and *May Lucas;* "Tobasco" for *Serpentine Butterfly*. But the Kinetophone was short-lived. Word had reached Edison of large screen projection taking place in Europe, and the Kinetophone was soon eclipsed by the Projecting Vitascope, the large-screen projection system acquired by Edison to contend with foreign competition. The synchronization of sound was placed on the inventor's back burner. Edison produced a few synchronized sound films from 1912 to 1914, some of them capturing musical performances. But the enterprise was not financially successful, and he abandoned the project.

Music was also vital to the birth of motion pictures in Europe. The first films in France and Germany were projected onto large screens and shown to communal audiences. These screenings were either accompanied by music—or were soon to be. But unlike Edison's peep-show device, these screenings used live music. In 1892 in Paris, Émile Reynaud showed *Pantomimes lumineuses,* a series of animated projections, to music composed for the occasion by Gaston Paulin. In December 1895, the Lumière brothers would famously introduce their *cinématographe* to the public; the record is unclear about whether music was there at that first screening. But if it was not, it soon materialized at subsequent Lumière screenings in the form of live piano accompaniment by Emile Maraval. In November 1895, Max Skladanowsky in Berlin beat the Lumières to the punch by almost two months. For his presentations of filmed acrobats, dancers, boxers, and animal acts, Skladanowsky used a combination of original compositions and preexisting music performed live, an intriguing mix of polkas, gallops, waltzes, and marches. For instance, a selection from Mikhail Glinka's symphonic poem *Kamarinskaya* is supposed to have accompanied the Russian dancers. At the first screenings of the *cinématographe* in London in 1896, patrons recalled, variously, a piano and a harmonium. A command performance for Queen Victoria used a theater orchestra.

As film wended its way across Europe and indeed around the world, music followed it in both recorded and live forms. While the Edison company may have suggested specific phonograph recordings for use in its Kinetophones, there is no evidence to suggest that either Edison or the Lumières included instructions for the performance of live musical accompaniment when they exported their motion pictures abroad. And yet music found its way into screenings, if not immediately then within days, weeks, or months of the arrival of film in most places around the world. It is as if film exerted a gravitational pull toward music, in one form or another, no matter where films were screened.

Early on, phonograph recordings were an important source of musical accompaniment. Where such technology was available, it was often used to lure audiences for whom hearing the phonograph might have been as novel an experience as seeing moving images. Edison's Kinetoscopes appeared in London in 1894, and shortly thereafter enterprising individuals rigged phonographs to them to provide musical accompaniment. By 1896 Oskar Messter had used phonograph recordings to accompany films in Berlin; Edison's Kinetophones had appeared in Nizhniy Novgorod, Russia; and the first moving images in the Czech territories had been accompanied by phonograph recordings. In Prague, phonographs were equipped with oversized horns so they could be heard throughout an auditorium. Within a few short years, phonograph recordings were used in many places across Europe, and by 1903 a cinema in Brussels was devoted exclusively to phonographic sound, showcasing short films of operatic performances. As late as 1929 Luis Bunuel and Salvatore Dali's avant-garde film, *Un chien andalou*, was accompanied in Paris by phonograph records of tangos and excerpts from Wagnerian opera. There are accounts of phonographic accompaniment in Poland, Australia, and Mexico. In Iran, phonographic accompaniment had a particularly long history, lasting through the 1920s.

In the United States, phonograph recordings would become an increasingly important part of film exhibition with the development of nickelodeons, ca. 1905–07, converted storefronts in urban neighborhoods dedicated to screening films. Nickelodeons presented a varied program of moving pictures, variety acts, illustrated songs (slides with illustrations and lyrics so the audiences could sing along), and musical performances with various forms of musical accompaniment including phonograph recordings. Often the phonograph would be positioned outside the nickelodeon, doing double duty as ballyhoo to lure passersby and as accompaniment for the show inside.

Although the use of phonograph recordings was an important characteristic of silent film exhibition, live musical accompaniment was the more common form. Before the nickelodeon, live accompaniment was typical of film exhibition in the United States, where films screened in variety show venues such as vaudeville. Musicians in the pit orchestra played for the moving images as they had for the live performers on the program. Edison's Projecting Vitascope premiered in 1896 at one such venue, Koster and Bial's Music Hall, in New York City. By 1904 theaters in Europe devoted exclusively to film were providing live musical accompaniment—in Denmark with a pianist, and in Stockholm with a small ensemble of musicians. Live music materialized at screenings of moving images in places as diverse as India, Iran, Japan, China, Hong Kong, Australia, New Zealand, Mexico, and Brazil.

Musical accompaniment around the world

In the first decade of film history, music proved central to the experience of film around the world. But different film traditions in various countries devised differing approaches to musical accompaniment. In the United States and Western Europe, popular music as well as art music could be heard. Many countries gravitated toward their own indigenous music, both traditional and popular. In Russia, for instance, many accompanists depended upon native Russian music and often paid no attention to the image track as they performed it. Russian audiences, it appears, were not dismayed. Musical accompaniment could function as a powerful medium of cultural dissemination, and it would play an increasingly important role in this capacity as the silent period progressed.

In India, Lumière's *cinématographe* was shown in Bombay (now Mumbai) in July 1896. It is likely that the earliest screenings were silent. Given the strong tradition of indigenous song and dance in Indian theater, it is not surprising that live musical accompaniment quickly found its way into Indian cinemas. By August 1896 the *Times of India* reported that appropriate music accompanied performances. Accompanists often served as lecturers too, a role sometimes taken by singers who narrated in song form. Traditionally, English films would be screened with popular Western songs played on Western instruments, while locally produced Indian films would be accompanied by classical rāgas and folk songs played on traditional Indian instruments such as the tabla (a drum), the sarangi (a bowed lute), and harmonium, adapted for use in India with drone stops. There is evidence, however, that these two traditions sometimes intersected: violins and clarinets were heard along with Indian instruments during Indian films, and the sarangi was heard with Western instruments during English films.

In Iran, the first films may have been the home movies made of the Shah's European trip in 1900. Soon motion pictures became a leisure activity of royalty and the upper classes. When the first public cinema opened in Tehran in 1904, films screened there were virtually all foreign, imported from the West, and lecturer-translators could be heard along with live musical accompaniment utilizing Western music and instruments, often piano and violin. Phonograph recordings from the West were also heard during screenings, reminding us that in many places throughout the world, recorded and live musical accompaniment were equally available options. That first theater in Tehran soon closed, but others eventually took its place. As cinema-going developed in Iran, theaters drawing upon lower-class audiences opened, but here Persian music played before, after, and during films.

In Japan, the Kinetoscope, Vitascope, and *cinématographe* had all arrived by 1897. Early on, exhibitors used bands playing on barges near viewing spaces to advertise the screenings and provide background music for them. Soon, musical accompaniment was performed by small orchestras positioned behind the audience. The subject matter of many of the earliest Japanese-produced films centered around music. In 1899 in Tokyo, films of geisha dancers were presented on the bill in variety-show theaters where it is hard to imagine that the musicians in the pit orchestra did not provide some form of musical accompaniment. By 1908 some theaters employed a full orchestra and live singers for film screenings.

In Japan, as in India, musical accompaniment to screenings of foreign films utilized Western instruments and melodies, often derived from opera. Accompaniment for films produced in Japan, however, utilized traditional Japanese music and instruments such as the shamisen (a three-stringed banjo) and taiko drums. (As Junko Ogihara has shown, theaters in Los Angeles's Little Tokyo continued the tradition of accompanying Japanese films with traditional Japanese music and instruments.) In practice, however, evidence suggests that musical accompaniment was sometimes a hybrid of the two practices, mixing traditional Japanese and Western musical elements during performances of both foreign and locally produced films.

In China and Hong Kong, music similarly proved central to the experience of film. In Shanghai, the first films were shown in 1896. Edison's Vitascope debuted in May 1897; by July of that year the local newspaper noted live piano accompaniment. The first indigenously produced films in Peking (now Beijing), *Dingjun Mountain* (1905), and in Hong Kong, *Stealing a Roast Duck* (1909), were of performances drawn from famous Chinese operas. *Dingjun Mountain* was supposedly shot with live music on the set, and it seems likely that selections from the operatic source were reproduced by local musicians on native instruments when the film was screened.

Japanese *benshi* and the role of the lecturer

The tradition of the lecturer was as integral a part of the Japanese cinema as musical accompaniment. Called *benshi,* these lecturers explicated and interpreted moving pictures for audiences, and their appearance roughly coincides with the arrival of cinema in Japan in 1896. Many of the benshi were already stars of the Kabuki theater or became stars for their film work, many with devoted followings among film audiences. The power of the benshi was such that musicians accompanying the films had to coordinate with benshi so that music would not compete with the benshi's voice. Lecturers/translators were an important feature of the film experience in many countries, including the United States. Their presence interacted with and sometimes substituted for musical accompaniment. In the cases of Brazil and India, lecturers provided both, singing their commentary.

The earliest indigenous Brazilian films have not survived, but their titles, such as *Dance of a Bahian* (1899) and *Capoeira Dance* (1905) allude to Bahia, an Afro-Brazilian community, and the music produced there. Again, it is hard to imagine that these dance films were shown without some attempt at re-creating Afro-Brazilian music such as the samba. Brazilian filmmakers mined Brazilian popular music and musical performers throughout the silent era, sometimes synchronizing showings with live singers behind the screen.

With this veritable explosion of varied musical accompaniments, it is important to note that some films screened in silence. Edison's Kinetoscope films were unaccompanied by music, and even projected Vitascope films were sometimes screened without music. Rick Altman has made the case that the first screenings of Edison's Projecting Vitascope at Koster and Bial's did not use the music described in newspaper accounts to accompany the films, but rather to introduce them. In Russia it took more than a decade for musical accompaniment in any form to assert itself and some films, perhaps even into the 1910s, screened in silence. Even in the United States, Altman's research has shown, silence was not uncommon.

Music and moving image existed in a complex relationship in the first decade of film history. Some films screened in silence, but most films were accompanied by music of some kind. Some music was provided by phonograph recordings, but most was live. Live accompaniment could mean a single musician, often a pianist, a small ensemble of players, or a theater orchestra. Some musical accompaniment was intermittent, some was continuous. Some accompaniment was improvised, and that improvisation may or may not have responded to the events on screen. Some accompaniment was originally composed for a specific film even in this early period, but most exploited preexisting music. Indigenous music, both traditional and contemporary, proved a staple throughout the world. This diversity underscores the fact that the earliest examples of musical accompaniment did not reflect a single, unifying practice.

Music and the birth of an art form

Beginning around 1906 and continuing through the 1910s, the film business is characterized by efforts to stabilize the fledging industry as a profitable enterprise and establish its legitimacy as an art form. These efforts included the development of a narrative-based medium (such as the classical narrative tradition in the United States) and the expansion of film length (ultimately culminating in the 60- to 120-minute feature-length film); the evolution and standardization of film technology and the development of techniques to facilitate a narrative-based medium; the upgrading of film content (such as the adaptations of literary and stage classics by the *Film d'Art* company in France or the filming of Kabuki troupes in Japan); the gentrification of viewing spaces evolving into the elaborate picture palaces of the 1910s and 1920s; and the attraction of larger audiences. Musical accompaniment was a critical part of this transformation. Attempts to encourage the appropriate and continuous presence of live accompaniment and to police its quality originate at this time. It would not be long before the quality of musical accompaniment would be a factor that exhibitors touted to market their theaters.

A number of institutions and practices fostered this transformation. Trade publications addressed music, disseminating techniques, setting standards, and advocating the live and continuous presence of music. In France, Gaumont began circulating a weekly *Guide Musicale* to exhibitors as early as 1907, and in the United States, "Incidental Music for Edison Pictures" appeared in the *Edison Kinetograms* beginning in 1909. Other studios, trade publications, and entrepreneurs also began making suggestions for suitable types of music. Evolving throughout the 1910s, the cue sheet (as it came to be known) was a list of musical pieces designed to help accompanists create a seamless and appropriate score. In the United States, selections culled from a variety of sources including standards of the concert hall, especially nineteenth-century art music, popular and folk tunes, and original compositions, were cued to specific moments in a film. Later, cue sheets derived from original scores were circulated in locations where orchestral resources were limited, a reminder that throughout the silent era, the same films could be heard with different music in different venues.

Cue sheets often circulated with films as they traversed the globe. In China, accompanists had access to these cue sheets and apparently used them for screenings of foreign films. As cue sheets evolved, they became more elaborate including excerpts from musical selections, timings, and intricate directions for coordinating music and image. Cue sheets depended upon the numerous musical encyclopedias, which began to be published at roughly the same time.

Musical encyclopedias contained inventories of music, some originally composed for use in the cinema and some preexisting, catalogued by their narrative utility. Among the most influential were Giuseppi Becce's *Kinothek* series published in Berlin (1919–29), J. S. Zamecnik's *Sam Fox Moving Picture Music* series (1913–14), and Erno Rapee's *Motion Picture Moods for Pianists and Organists* (1924) and *Encyclopedia of Music for Pictures* (1925), published in the United States. These encyclopedias extensively catalogued narrative situations accompanists might face and suggested appropriate music. Zamecnik's "Indian Music," for instance, provides an all-purpose cue for the presence of American Indians on screen.

Zamecnik's "Hurry Music" was customized for struggles, duels, and mob or fire scenes. Even treachery was adapted for villains, ruffians, smugglers, or conspirators. Rapee's *Encyclopedia* had dozens of categories offering music from battles to weddings (and most everything in between). Musical encyclopedias in one form or another were used worldwide. In Japan, accompanists were provided with catalogues of mood music; in Russia, Anatoli Goldobin and Boris Azancheyev published *Accompanying Cinematograph Pictures on the Piano* (1912).

Much of the music of the silent era has been lost or was never written down so that much of what we know about the form and character of silent film accompaniment comes from the surviving discourses surrounding early film music: cue sheets, encyclopedias, advice columns in trade publications, newspaper reviews, how-to manuals, and oral histories. These sources help us to reconstruct how music functioned in the silent era. Unfortunately, access to these resources is limited. There is much work left to be done uncovering resources around the globe, and as a result we have a less-than-complete picture of music's functioning in the silent era.

1. J. S. Zamecnik's *Moving Picture Music*, vol. 1 (1913) was one of a number of influential musical encyclopedias published in the silent era. "Indian Music" is typical of the generic approach of these encyclopedias, and the "tom-tom" rhythm in the bass clef is based on stereotypes about Native American musical performance.

From the sources that we do have, we can see that by the 1910s, in the United States and Western Europe film music had gravitated toward providing a few functions: identifying geographic location and time period; intensifying mood; delineating emotion; illustrating onscreen action; and fleshing out characterization.

Accompanists came to rely on musical conventions (some might say clichés) to do so such as tremolo for suspense, pizzicato for sneakiness, and dissonance for villainy. In fact, mood music became so central to silent film accompaniment that it was often played on the set to motivate the actors during filming.

As musical accompaniment began to coalesce around these functions, the use of popular music was beginning to chafe against them. Popular music served a key role in silent film exhibition. Publications on musical accompaniment in the United States and Western Europe, however, were beginning to advocate its limited use and decried the practice of selecting popular songs based on the appropriateness of their titles. Consider the trouble that one of the most influential music directors of the era experienced in trying to rid cinema of popular music in New York. Erno Rapee, a preeminent film music composer and conductor, and the author of two important encyclopedias of film music, frequently complained about the audience's preference for popular music. Rapee made it a personal crusade to introduce art music into film accompaniment, but he was not entirely successful in doing so. Hollywood saw the handwriting on the wall, and by the 1920s many studios began promoting songs composed expressly for their films and buying music publishing houses to market them.

Studies on the impact of race and ethnicity on film reception similarly underscore the centrality of popular music and the trouble it could cause. Mary Carbine's research has shown that in Chicago's African American community, where Fats Waller and Louis Armstrong once played in theater orchestras, blues and jazz accompanied screenings for black audiences of films produced for white audiences. Armstrong noted how the musicians ignored what was transpiring on screen when the playing heated up, a practice that generated complaints from some audience members who found such unmotivated accompaniment distracting. Popular music during this era—its various practices and the discourses surrounding it—remind us that musical accompaniment could function transgressively and thus become a potential site of cultural struggle.

It is interesting to speculate on how much of this transgressive potential was tapped in other places. As we have seen, in many countries where national cinemas developed, indigenous popular musics were incorporated into filmic accompaniment for films produced locally. Here music becomes an expressive gesture toward national identity. But indigenous music was also incorporated into the accompaniment of foreign films in India, Iran, and Japan, and perhaps many other places. I am reminded of the early Japanese film entrepreneur Toyojiro Takamatsu, who traveled around Japan screening films. For the foreign films, Takamatsu provided voice-over mistranslation, transforming films, no matter what their original content, into examples of his own socialist politics. We need more research to flesh out exactly what happened when indigenous music was heard during screenings of foreign films. To what extent did such music transform or even critique film content? Music mediates the reception of films and can challenge the technologies, values, and narratives tied up in them. The power of music as a point of cultural interface in silent film exhibition, indeed a potential site of resistance, is an entire field that needs to be explored.

While popular music was being exploited, film scores commissioned for specific films began to emerge. Although examples exist as early as the 1890s, the phenomenon can be traced to the French *Film d'Art* company, which yoked prestige productions to film scores by prominent art music composers. Camille Saint-Saën's score for *L'Assassinat du Duc de Guise* (1908) is the best surviving example. At the same time in Russia, Mikhail Ippolitov-Ivanov scored *Stenka Razin* (1908), and somewhat later in Italy, Pietro Mascagni scored *Satan's Rhapsody* (1915). These scores, for the most part, did not accompany films outside their country of origin.

In the United States, originally composed scores begin appearing as early as 1910. Martin Marks has uncovered more than one hundred scores used between 1911 and 1913 alone, many of them for the Kalem Company. His illuminating work on the Joseph Carl Breil and D. W. Griffith score for *The Birth of a Nation* (1915) is among the first examples of film music scholarship of that period. For an early silent film score with its original music, there is *Cabiria* (1914), an Italian superspectacle more than two hours long, restored on DVD with the original score by Manlio Mazza heard in a piano reduction.

By "original" I mean the historically specific score commissioned for an individual film. Although original to the film, such scores are not original in the way we might suppose them to be. Rather they are often compilations, cobbled together from a variety of sources and sometimes including newly composed material. Breil and Griffith's influential score for *The Birth of a Nation*, while original to that film, is a compilation of such symphonic chestnuts as Richard Wagner's "Ride of the Valkyries" and Edvard Grieg's "In the Hall of the Mountain King" as well as patriotic tunes, popular songs, minstrel music, and some new composition, notably a love theme supposedly penned by Griffith himself.

Richard Wagner exerted an influence on film accompanists from the beginning. His theory of the *gesamtkunstwerk* (total art work) provided a model for the ways in which music could be attentive to the drama, and his use of the leitmotif became a model for unifying the accompaniment and clarifying the story. As early as 1910, a cue sheet for the Edison company's *Frankenstein* uses a theme from Carl Maria von Weber's opera *Der Freischűtz* as a leitmotif for the monster. Russian newspapers reported that Khudyakov's "melodic themes" for *The Terrible Vengeance* (1913) "fitted the characters perfectly." *Moving Picture News* in the United States reported in 1910 that the use of the leitmotif is a "natural law that must on no account be broken." Still, Wagnerian principles were not universally adopted. Mazza, for instance, did not use leitmotifs in the score for *Cabiria*.

2. The Spencer organ at the Tivoli Opera House in San Francisco with Earl Abel at the keyboard. During the silent era, the elaborate theater organ was an instrument capable of producing a huge sound and a multiplicity of sound effects.

By the 1920s, audiences in the United States and Europe came to expect a preplanned, largely nonimprovisatory, continuous musical accompaniment responding in some way to screen content and performed at a certain level of expertise. The piano may have been the workhorse of the era, but the theater organ was the star.

The Mighty Wurlitzer, developed specifically for film accompaniment, was the gold standard in the United States with numerous theatrical stops to create sound effects. One of its many competitors, the Morton Pipe Organ, boasted a telephone ring, door knocks, church and sleigh bells, steamboat, train, police and bird whistles, car horns, fire gongs, surf, wind, thunder, horse hooves, airplane motors, castanets, and Chinese gongs. In large cities, motion picture orchestras provided accompaniment in

3. The Capitol was one of New York's premier movie theaters, and it boasted first-class orchestral accompaniment. Here, David Mendoza conducts the Capitol Grand Orchestra.

palatial theaters built exclusively for film. The Roxy Theater in New York boasted an orchestra of more than one hundred players. Some conductors even rivaled a film's director in name recognition.

The apex of the silent film score

The 1920s witnessed the great flowering of the film score. Music was specifically created for many films of the late silent era including *Nosferatu* (1922), scored by Hans Erdmann; *Metropolis* (1927), scored by Gottfried Huppertz; *La Roue* (1923), scored by Arthur Honegger; *Broken Blossoms* (1919), scored by Louis F. Gottschalk; and *The Thief of Bagdad* (1924), scored by Mortimer Wilson. Cutting-edge composition could be heard in Edmund Meisel's atonal score for *Battleship Potemkin* (1925), blamed for causing riots at the Berlin premiere and banned; in George Antheil's dissonant score for *Ballet mécanique* (1924); and in Erik Satie's convention-defying score for *Entr'acte* (1924). In Argentina, screenings of *La muchacha del arrabal* (1922) were accompanied by tangos, with lyrics penned by the film's director, José Ferreyra. In Iran, Ebrahim Moradi composed a score for his silent film *Bolhavas* (1933) and apparently attempted some form of synchronization when the score was performed live with the silent projection.

Satie's *Entr'acte* score is one of the most intriguing of the era. About twenty minutes in length, *Entr'acte*, directed by Rene Clair, was intended to be screened between the two acts of a ballet as part of a performance promoted as an evening of anarchy. A Dadaist attack on rationality and logic, *Entr'acte* was meant to embody pure cinema, bereft of the encumbrance of narrative and inspired by the dream. Like Clair, who defied the developing conventions of narrative cinema (or tried to), Satie turned his back on conventions of musical accompaniment by undercutting the use of music to respond to the images, avoiding the use of leitmotifs or any unifying structure, confounding clear rhythms, and even resisting tonality itself. For instance, although sections of the score seem nominally to revolve around tonal harmony, it seems to move from the unrelated keys of A major to F major to C major in the opening section, with a striking absence of clear tonic chords to reinforce these keys. There are, in fact, so many unresolved dissonances that whatever chords we do hear are stripped of their function to anchor a stable harmonic system. There is, however, one example of a solid tonic chord in the score. In a bit of wonderful comic subterfuge, the word *fin* (French for "the end") appears on the screen. But the film, it turns out, is not over, and a performer motions us not to leave accompanied by the only moment of finality in the score—a major triad!

Silent film has been enjoying a resurgence in recent years. Inaugurated in the 1970s by PBS television broadcasts of silent films with scores by William Perry, by silent film screenings with live accompaniment by scholar/conductor Gillian Anderson in the United States and Carl Davis in Britain, and by high profile performances in the 1980s of Carmine Coppola's score for

Napoleon (1929), the rebirth of silent film has made it possible for audiences today to feel something of the all-encompassing experience that characterized film in the 1920s. Many scores have been lost, such as Darius Milhaud's legendary score for *L 'Inhumaine* (1924), but some have been found. In 1975, Dmitri Shostakovich's lost score for *The New Babylon* (1929) was discovered and in the early 1980s was performed live with the film across Europe and in the United States. More and more silent films are being rescued from oblivion, and music is becoming a key component of their restoration. Some restorations have reconstructed the original scores: *Broken Blossoms* (1919); *Nosferatu* (1922); *Metropolis* (1927); and *The Man With a Movie Camera* (1929) for which the Alloy Orchestra created a score from Dziga Vertov's original musical instructions. Sadly, *Broken Blossoms* and *The Man With a Movie Camera* are no longer available on DVD with their original scores. Other restorations feature newly composed scores: Carl Davis's for *The Wind* (1928); the Alloy Orchestra's for *Strike* (1925); the Clubfoot Orchestra's for *Sherlock Jr.* (1924); jazz trombonist Wycliffe Gordon's for *Body and Soul* (1925); Michael Nyman's for *The Man With a Movie Camera;* Joseph Turrin's for *Broken Blossoms*; and Robert Israel's for *La Roue* (1923). Even some of these are no longer available. A fascinating curiosity is the 1975 score for the Japanese surrealist film *A Page of Madness* (1927), composed by its director Teinsoke Kinugasa when the film was rediscovered nearly fifty years after its initial release. Georgio Moroder notoriously used disco in the 1985 restoration of *Metropolis,* and the British band The Pet Shop Boys scored *Battleship Potemkin* and performed it live for a screening in London's Trafalgar Square in 2004. In 2000 Turner Classic Movies launched the Young Composers Competition in which finalists compete for the opportunity to score a full-length silent film, which is subsequently broadcast nationally. But the most exciting development is the continued success of silent films screened with live musical accompaniment at film festivals and archives, in concert halls, and sometimes even in the very places where they were first heard: film theaters.

Chapter 5
A history of film music II: 1927–1960

The quest for synchronization and its realization long preceded the worldwide conversion to sound. As we have seen, W. K. L. Dickson at Edison achieved synchronization of music and image as early as 1894. Oskar Messter in Germany, Léon Gaumont in France, Cecil Hepworth in England, and Kazimierz Proszynski in Poland also devised sound systems for large-screen projection, all of which involved the synchronization of phonographs and projectors. These systems were hounded by problems: the phonograph's limited capacity for amplification; the restricted length and poor sound quality of recordings; problems in synchronization between phonographs and projectors; and substantial start-up costs. By the 1920s competing technologies in the United States and Germany had solved these problems either by perfecting the sound-on-disc approach (Vitaphone in the United States) or creating sound-on-film systems with sound optically printed on the film itself (Tri-Ergon in Germany and Phonofilm in the United States). Inventors in the Soviet Union and Japan would not be far behind.

The conversion to sound and the role of popular song

Music played a key role in what happened next. In an attempt to get an edge on the competition, Warner Bros. invested in

Vitaphone to upgrade the musical accompaniment for its films. The New York Philharmonic was hired to record the score for the studio's first Vitaphone feature, *Don Juan* (1926), which screened with loudspeakers positioned in the orchestra pit. Al Jolson's ad-libbed patter in Warner Bros.' next Vitaphone feature, a musical titled *The Jazz Singer* (1927), ushered in the sound revolution. Although it was dialogue that drove the new technology, it was the genre of the musical that that most fully exploited it. In the United States, important refinements in sound production were developed in musicals—postsynchronization in *Hallelujah* (1929) and double-channel recording and postrecording in *Applause* (1929). Some of the earliest successful sound films in Europe were musicals: *The Blue Angel* (1930) in Germany; *Le Million* (1931) in France; *Evergreen* (1934) in England. Musicals proved so profitable in the United States and abroad that even in nonmusical genres it was common to include songs, which studios marketed through sheet music and recordings.

The performance of indigenous song and dance was quickly embraced worldwide as a showcase for the new sound technology and a platform for the expression of national culture. The integrated musicals developing in Hollywood, where production numbers advanced the narrative, were an important influence throughout Latin America where the genre was customized with local musics: the *tangueras* of Argentina (*Adiós Buenos Aires*, 1938); the *chanchadas* of Brazil, with roots in Carnaval and the Afro-Brazilian samba (*Alô Alô Carnaval*, 1936); and the *comedias rancheros* of Mexico, which made prominent use of mariachis (*Allá en el Rancho Grande*, 1936). In the 1940s, during the Golden Age of Mexican cinema, popular indigenous songs were interpolated into melodramas such as Emilio Fernández's *María Candalaria* (1944) and *Flor Silvestre* (1943).

Even in the Stalinist-era Soviet Union, the integrated musical was an important genre, although any connection to the Hollywood musical with its decadent connotations was downplayed. Depending upon established stars of the recording industry and infused with Soviet ideology, musicals set on rural collectives such as *The Tractor Drivers* (1939), or in urban settings such as *The Happy Guys* (1934), incorporated the performance of original songs, Soviet military and patriotic songs, and folk music.

Popular and folk songs were also inserted into nonmusical genres in the Soviet Union. It is interesting to consider the interpolation of the popular songs "How Good Life Will Be" and "If Only I Had Mountains of Gold" into such politically charged dramas as *Alone* (1931) and *Golden Mountains* (1931) or the impressive choruses in the historical epic *Alexander Nevsky* (1938) in the context of the immense popularity of Soviet musicals. Song, both in and out of musicals, would prove a distinctive feature of Soviet films for decades to come.

Integrated Hollywood-type musicals did not materialize in China, although something close to that model did emerge in Hong Kong later in the century. This is not to say that song was not an important facet of the first sound films in China; songs were interpolated into a variety of different genres, often involving actors who could sing. Chinese opera would prove a particularly durable musical source, and the first sound film in China, *The Songstress Red Peony* (1931), used four songs from Chinese opera, dubbed by the opera master Mei Lanfang, famous for his portrayals of female characters on the opera stage. In the 1930s, leftist filmmakers would insert revolutionary songs alongside those from opera in films such as *Big Road* (1935) and *Street Angel* (1937). In *Street Angel*, the audience is invited to sing along to lyrics on the screen. In Hong Kong, early sound films such as *White Golden Dragon* (1933) mined Chinese opera for stories, stars, and, of course, music. The first Taiwanese sound film was also based in opera, *Six Talents' Romance of the West Chamber* (1955). Indigenous song, either borrowed from Chinese opera or the popular repertoire, or originally composed in traditional or popular idioms, filled the soundtracks of Chinese-language films and produced some of the most popular songs of the twentieth century in China, Hong Kong, and Taiwan.

Song was central to the development of sound film. But, as we have seen in Chinese-language films, the use of song in many parts of the world was so different from that of Hollywood that we need to re-examine the utility of generic constructs like the musical outside the West. The film industry in India provides an even more dramatic case. The powerful traditions of song and dance in nineteenth-century Indian theater paved the way for the use of music in the silent era when live singers could sometimes be heard providing accompaniment. Sound films became saturated with song, some with more than fifty musical numbers! These early sound films were produced by various regional film industries and in various dialects—*Alam Ara* (1931) in Hindi; *Kalidasa* (1931) in Tamil; and *Bhakta Prahlad* (1931) in Telegu—and songs within the films were performed in a variety of languages—Tamil, Telegu, Hindi, Bengali, and Sanskrit. The performance of indigenous song became a defining part of the film landscape throughout India but especially in Hindi cinema, centered in Bombay (now Mumbai) and sometimes called Bollywood, where it became a virtual requirement to include multiple performances of song (and dance) in every film regardless of genre.

In the process, a hybrid and synthetic musical form was forged, the film song, influenced by classical Indian Karnatic and Hindustani rãgas, popular folk musics, and Western harmonic influences, and a new way of performing it, with playback singers, popular artists who prerecorded the songs to be lip-synched by the actors. Many of the playback singers, particularly Lata Mangeshkar and her sister Asha Bhosle (who claims to have recorded more than 12,000 songs), developed enormous fan bases, becoming more popular than the actors. Lata Mangeshkar, who began her career in 1948, continues her immense popularity to this day.

Composers of film songs, known as music directors, were featured prominently in a film's advertising and were often paid more than the director. Important music directors in early sound film include C. Ramchandra, who drew upon traditional music from the Uttar Pradesh region and mixed it with Western swing, jazz, and Latin American rhythms; the team of Shankar-Jaikashan, who worked from the 1950s until the 1980s; and Saraswati Devi, the first woman music director who joined Bombay Talkies Film Company in 1935 and sustained a successful career in music inside and outside the studio until the 1950s.

The first film songs were performed by small ensembles comprised of many of same instruments that were used in the silent era including the harmonium and tabla. By the 1930s the violin, cello, mandolin, piano, organ, and clarinet were added as well as Indian instruments including the veena, *pakhawaj*, *jal tarang*, *bansuri*, and sitar. By the 1950s, studio orchestras expanded to more than one hundred players. Film songs were so important to Hindi cinema that they came first in the production process: the job of the screenwriter was to provide a narrative framework upon which to hang these songs. This process of fitting the narrative to the songs became known as picturization.

Hindi cinema gave rise to a new model for including song, different from the way song became institutionalized in Hollywood and leading to some fundamental differences in the reception of film itself. Hindi cinema, and many other national cinemas like it, invert the relationship between narrative exposition and performance central to the integrated Hollywood musical where narrative is prioritized, and songs are integrated into the storyline. In Hindi cinema, the songs are prioritized and the narrative operates in relation to them with storylines picturizing the songs. Further, in the Hollywood musical, the technologies of song performance (prerecording, dubbing, postdubbing) are carefully hidden so as not to disturb the illusion of reality. In Hindi cinema, the technology is exposed. Songs are not sung by the onscreen characters but dubbed by playback singers, a fact well known by audiences, producing a distinctly different form of cinematic pleasure from that on offer from Hollywood, one not contingent upon a suspension of disbelief and hinging instead on cinema's artifice.

For a significant portion of the world, Bollywood is much more characteristic of the way music developed in sound film than is Hollywood. Many national cinemas in Asia and Africa share with Hindi cinema similar assumptions about the centrality of indigenous music and the relationship of narrative and performance. The first Persian sound films were actually produced in Bombay. *The Lor Girl* (1932) included Persian singing and dancing to original songs composed expressly for the film. *Film Farsi* developed after World War II in Iran incorporating song and dance in genre-benders that mixed action film, melodrama, and comedy, such as the box-office success *Sharmsar* (1950) starring Delkash, a popular Iranian songstress. Soon, the performances of songs were dubbed by popular singers, as they were in Hindi cinema, and actors established relationships with singers who would provide their onscreen voices. In fact, in the postwar era, the inclusion of Persian singing and dancing became so obligatory that foreign films were altered to meet the expectations of Persian audiences. Thus when the Hollywood blockbuster *Ben-Hur* (1959) was screened, songs performed by Iranian singers were interpolated into the film.

Egypt quickly developed into one of the largest film industries in the Arab world, and as in the Hindi industry, the performance of song was a crucial element. Films of various genres with interpolated musical performances constituted a significant portion of the industry's output and commercial successes well into the 1960s. Song and dance were important facets of Egyptian culture long before sound film arrived, and Egyptian cinema had a number of popular performers it could tap for its growing industry. The musical melting pot that produced the Egyptian film song—Latin American rhythms, themselves influenced by African music, Western instrumentation and song structure, and traditional Arab song—can be heard in films such as *The White Rose* (1934) and *Wedad* (1936), which made film stars of the popular singers and recording artists Mohamed Abdel-Wahab and Umm Kulthum. In *Victory of Youth* (1941) and *Honeymoon* (1946) Lebanese and Syrian musical elements were added to the mix. Among the most popular postwar Egyptian films were love stories told against a background of musical performances in such films as *The Flirtation of Girls* (1949) with the popular singer Layla Murad.

When several Arab film industries began incorporating musical performances later in the twentieth century, they modeled their films on this Egyptian model: in Lebanon, *The Seller of the Rings* (1965), *Safar Barlek* (1966), and *The Daughter of the Guardian* (1968); in Morocco, *Life Is a Struggle* (1968) and *Silence Is a One-Way Street* (1973); and in Tunisia, *Screams* (1972). Philippe Aractingi's recent Lebanese film *Bosta* (2005) incorporates folk music and dance, which it juxtaposes with the disruptive force of European techno music.

The performance of song generated a number of different practices in early sound film. Background music followed a similar trajectory. Background music—what is traditionally called the score—refers to the music playing in the background, that is, not foregrounded in the film through performance or visually produced within the film. Different film practices treated background music in different ways: from Hindi cinema, where background music was so overshadowed by film songs that the composers who created it were often uncredited, to Soviet cinema, where principles of montage were applied to the score; from Chinese-language film and *Film Farsi,* where *bricolage* construction mixed a variety of musical sources, to the Hollywood studio system, which generated a highly codified institutional practice for the composition and placement of background music.

The development of the background score

The initial response to the question of what to do about background music was characterized by diversity. There were some attempts to preserve silent traditions. Charlie Chaplin's early sound films, *City Lights* (1931) and *Modern Times* (1936), had virtually no dialogue or sound effects and were scored with continuous music. In Japan, the persistence of silent projection continued well into the 1930s promoted by benshi trying vainly to stave off synchronized sound and unemployment. Ironically, now that technology made possible the economical reproduction of first-class musical accompaniment, many films used no background music at all or went to absurd lengths to justify its presence. In Josef von Sternberg's otherwise gritty Hollywood crime drama, *Thunderbolt* (1929), prisoners just happen to be practicing music in their cells (von Suppe's *Poet and Peasant* no less) during the film's climactic escape sequence.

There were innovative responses, too. In Hollywood, Hugo Riesenfeld combined two different musical mediums, a jazz band and a small orchestra, for distinctive effects in *Sunrise* (1927). In France, Maurice Jaubert used electronic manipulation to produce an arresting cue for a slow-motion sequence in Jean Vigo's *Zéro de conduite* (1933). In the Netherlands, Hanns Eisler scored Joris Ivens's documentary *New Earth* (1934) using naturalistic sound for the machines but music for the humans. In Britain, Arthur Benjamin experimented with orchestration to compensate for problems in early sound recording, reducing the number of strings and even creating pizzicato effects from tuba and piano. And in Berlin, at the German Film Research Institute, filmic equivalents of musical phenomena were identified in order to facilitate synchronization between the two (such as the dolly-in and dolly-out for crescendo and decrescendo and superimpositions for dissonance). Perhaps it was these experiments that Arnold Schoenberg was thinking of when he was approached by Hollywood. The story goes that he was interested if he could complete the score first and the film be made to fit his music. (The answer was no.)

Very early in the sound period, composers in the Soviet Union treated the score as an element of montage. Influenced no doubt by the 1928 "Statement on Sound Film" (see chap. 2), Soviet filmmakers explored the emotional, intellectual, and ideological effects of music that created friction with the image. Believing that revolutionary art demands a revolutionary practice, Soviet filmmakers extended a revolutionary aesthetic to the score. In Pudovkin's *Deserter*, for instance, the despair and suicide of a starving worker caught stealing bread is alarmingly at odds with the jazzy melody and Latin-inflected rhythms of Yuri Shaporin's score. Earlier in the film, as contraband news is disseminated via newspapers, the jaunty background music starts and stops, as if a phonograph needle were arbitrarily picked up and dropped down. At the Communist party parade, shots of workers and soldiers are accompanied by a quotation from Bizet's *Carmen*. In Grigori Kozintsev and Leonid Trauberg's *Alone*, Dmitri Shostakovich scores a scene in which the heroine sobs out her agony to a party official with light-hearted, percussive music featuring a calliope-like street organ. In Serge Yutkevich's *Golden Mountains*, Shostakovich scores a sequence of men trampling through thick mud with the crisp sound of a xylophone and percussion, and accompanies unsympathetic bourgeoisie with Hawaiian guitars. Such musical and narrative disjunctions were designed to undercut conventional bourgeois emotional attachments on the part of the audience, opening up viewers to the revolutionary aesthetic of these early Soviet sound films.

In Japan, Akira Kurosawa was much influenced by Soviet filmmakers, and several of his postwar features are marked by examples of disjunctive uses of music: the shock effect of traditional Shinto music paired with Wagner's "Wedding March" during a Japanese bridal ceremony, or mamboesque pop music combined with a Buddhist monk's chanting at a funeral in *The*

Bad Sleep Well (1960); a jazzy saxophone riff accompanying bumbling medieval peasants in *The Hidden Fortress* (1958); a life-and-death telephone call accompanied by a tango or a tense confrontation between cop and criminal accompanied by a woman practicing a sonatina in *Stray Dog* (1949); or the use of the cheery "Cuckoo Waltz" assailing the gangster who has just learned he has lost a crucial power struggle in *Drunken Angel* (1948).

Another aesthetic was also shaping up in Japan. Although the first sound films depended upon popular songs to fill the soundtrack, composers from the concert hall such as Yamada Kosaku and Kami Kyosuke were soon drawn to film scoring. A lively debate ensued over the place of Western music. An important figure here is Fumio Hayasaka, who believed that films should incorporate Japanese music. His score for Mizoguchi's *Ugetsu* (1954) uses *geza* music of Kabuki theater, and his score for Mizoguchi's *The Crucified Lovers* (1954) features prominent use of Japanese percussion, fusing the boundary between music and sound. Hayasaka, memorably, scored a series of films for Kurosawa and sometimes found himself in conflict with the director over Kurosawa's fondness for Western-style music. For *Rashomon* (1950), Kurosawa insisted on a bolero, a Spanish dance form, but Hayasaka was also able to incorporate *gagaku*, traditional music of the Japanese Imperial Court performed on such traditional instruments as the *sho* (mouth organ) and the *wagon* (a type of zither).

In other places, a very different kind of practice developed for background music, one in which various kinds of music, both borrowed and originally composed, indigenous and foreign, converged in a kind of pastiche. These bricolage scores often fulfilled the functions common to silent film accompaniment, particularly the creation of mood and atmosphere. In Iran after World War II, the development of postsynchronization allowed film composers to create such scores from Persian music, original composition, Western art music, and Hollywood film scores.

Other Arab and African filmmaking traditions similarly exploited bricolage in the score combining Hollywood-style film music, indigenous music, both traditional and popular, and original composition. In the films of the Egyptian director Youssef Chahine, Hollywood-style background music was often used in calculated counterpoint to traditional Arab music. In *Always in My Heart* (1945), Egyptian director Salah Abu-Saif wove a folk song throughout the film as a leitmotif, and it became his signature tune in subsequent work.

In Shanghai, film music also gravitated toward bricolage. The composers Er Nie in *New Woman* (1935) and Luting He in *City Scenes* (1935) and *Street Angel* (1937) mixed Chinese folk and popular music with Western musical styles. It was not uncommon to hear Strauss waltzes, sacred music, US big band music, Latin American dance music, Chinese folk, traditional, and popular music along with originally composed music in the score. Although initially dismissed by critics as ineffectual, these early sound film scores have been reevaluated by scholars such as Sue Tuohy and Emilie (Yueh-yu) Yeh. They argue that these scores performed a critical role in envisioning China's future by juxtaposing, musically, China's past and its colonial present, creating a musical dialogue between East and West, often fraught with ambiguity, about social change.

In Hindi cinema, where film songs became a unique and enduring form of popular music and were marketed in advance of a film's release, the score itself was pushed into the background. Music directors composed the songs and, it was assumed, the background music, but often this was not the case as many composers toiled anonymously. Background music in Hindi cinema is built upon a bricolage of influences including traditional Indian musical elements and Western-style melodies and instrumentation.

The classical Hollywood film score

In the United States, a powerful model for the use of background music evolved in classical Hollywood cinema. This term refers to a practice for the production of narrative film institutionalized through a powerful studio system, which flourished from the 1930s through the early 1960s in and around Hollywood, California. As part of this practice, a set of conventions for the use of background music evolved in the 1930s, harnessing some of the most powerful effects of music not just to support the seamless storytelling that Hollywood perfected but also to engage the audience uncritically in the world that the story creates. The classical Hollywood film score revolved around a core set of functions: music to sustain unity by covering potential gaps in the narrative chain occasioned by editing (such as transitions between sequences and especially montages); music to emphasize narrative action through coordination of music and image, often through "mickey mousing," matching screen action explicitly to the rhythms and shape of the music (so named because it was distinctively developed in Disney cartoons); music to control connotation by fleshing out mood and atmosphere, establishing time and geographic place, and delineating characters' subjectivity; music to accompany dialogue, called *underscoring*, through the subordination of music to speech; and music to connect the audience to the filmic world through an appeal to emotion. Music was rendered unobtrusive by masking its entrances and exits, but it was none the less powerful because it was relegated to the perceptual background.

The classical Hollywood film score coalesced especially through the work of three composers in the 1930s, Max Steiner, Erich Wolfgang Korngold, and Alfred Newman, whose scores for *King Kong* (1933), *The Adventures of Robin Hood* (1938), and *Wuthering Heights* (1939) respectively are among the most accomplished in the form. They were joined by others, notably Dimitri Tiomkin, Miklós Rózsa, Bronislau Kaper, and Franz

Waxman. All but Newman had immigrated from Europe, many fleeing Hitler and the rise of fascism.

A key element in the classical Hollywood film score was its Romantic idiom. In the 1930s when scoring conventions

Erich Wolfgang Korngold and *The Adventures of Robin Hood*

Korngold's score for *The Adventures of Robin Hood* is a consummate example of classical scoring principles. Korngold evokes, without actually adopting, late medieval music (notably in the Banquet sequence in Nottingham Castle), recasting the inflections of English balladry into a Romantic tapestry via the Warner Bros. studio orchestra. But it is in his use of leitmotifs that Korngold is at his most brilliant. King Richard's leitmotif, which comes to stand for England itself, is first heard in the stable harmony of E♭ major. Richard is off on the Crusades, and throughout the film his leitmotif is heard through a series of variations in major and minor keys returning to E♭ major only upon Richard's dramatic reappearance in England. The leitmotif for the villainous Guy of Gisbourne is built upon the disquieting intervals of ascending major sevenths and minor ninths. The innocence of Maid Marian is characterized through simple harmonies and a delicate melody with a high degree of repetition. The Norman oppression leitmotif is built on dissonance (descending minor seconds). Leitmotifs also connect the characters to each other in interesting ways. The leitmotif for Robin and Marian, which functions as their love theme, grows out of King Richard's leitmotif (they share an opening ascending fifth), suggesting that Robin and Marian's love of king and country is what brings them together. It is Richard's leitmotif that we hear during a key sequence in which Robin and Marian begin to fall in love, and Richard's leitmotif that plays a major role in the balcony scene where the couple declares their love. Even more interesting are the links between Robin and Guy, notably the ascending sevenths and ninths that can be heard introducing Robin's leitmotif when he confronts Guy at Nottingham Castle, suggesting intriguing similarities between hero and villain. In *The Adventures of Robin Hood*, key elements of Western tonality are exploited in the leitmotivic plan for the score, contributing to the development of character and theme.

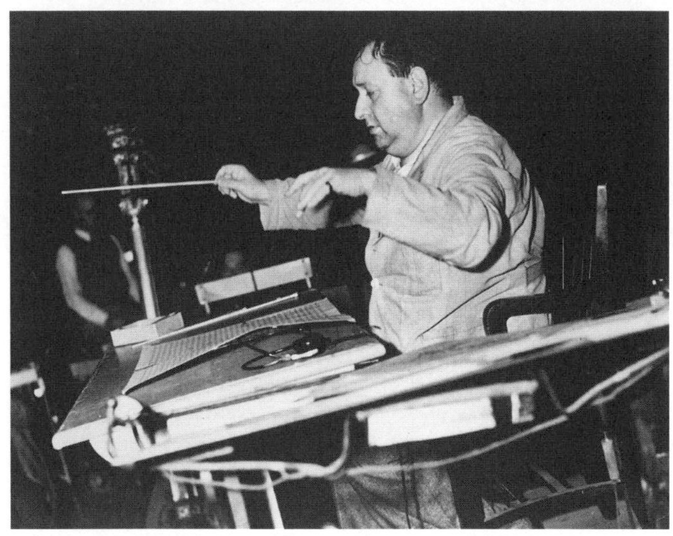

4. Erich Wolfgang Korngold, one of the architects of the classical Hollywood film score.

developed in Hollywood, Modernism was in full swing in concert halls and popular music was enjoying a surge of interest due to the growth of the radio and recording industries. And yet Romanticism was embraced as the vehicle for Hollywood to meet its musical needs. It is interesting to consider why. Romanticism privileges melody, an accessible musical structure for untrained listeners (as opposed to Baroque or Modern music), and the privileging of melody in the score meshed nicely with the privileging of narrative in classical Hollywood style. Romanticism also had at its disposal the concept of the leitmotif, an extremely adaptable mechanism for accessing listeners, unifying the score, and responding to a film's dramatic needs. Additionally, many of the influential scores of the silent era were already relying on Romantic models. I also think that the expanded size of the Romantic orchestra matched both Hollywood's grandiose conception of itself as well as the musical tastes of its producers. Many of the composers in Hollywood had been born in Europe at the end of the Romantic period and were trained in Romanticism. (But then, had Hollywood not been interested in Romanticism, it would not have attracted these composers.) Caryl Flinn theorizes that it was Hollywood's assembly-line mode of production and its accompanying artistic frustration that fostered Hollywood composers' attraction to Romanticism, with its focus on the individual and its belief in the transformative nature of creativity and art's transcendence over social and historical reality.

The Romantic idiom and its symphonic deployment have been utilized by many a composer working outside Hollywood (and by many lured to Hollywood) well into the twentieth century and beyond: William Walton for *Henry V* (1944) and Patrick Doyle for the 1999 remake in Great Britain; Nino Rota for *The Leopard* (1963) in Italy; Gabriel Yared for *Camille Claudel* (1988) in France. Even outside the West, the symphony orchestra and Romantic traditions have held a certain fascination and have been deployed, in combination with indigenous harmonics and instruments, by Zhao Jiping for *Red Firecracker, Green Firecracker* (1994) in the People's Republic of China; by Tan Dun for *Crouching Tiger, Hidden Dragon* (2000) in Taiwan; and by Tôru Takemitsu for *Ran* (1985) in Japan.

5. Muir Matheson conducts William Walton's score for *Hamlet* (1948). When film scores were recorded, the conductor watched the film projected on a giant screen behind the orchestra.

New musical vocabularies come to Hollywood

Romanticism began to be challenged for pride of place around mid-century when Hollywood composers began experimenting in the vocabularies of folk and jazz, the structuring model of Serialism, and the idioms of Modernism and Minimalism. While the classical Hollywood film score continued to influence the functions and placement of music, its expression was being updated. In the concert hall, composers such as Aaron Copland in *Appalachian Spring*, *Billy the Kid*, and *Rodeo*, and Virgil Thomson in *Symphony on a Hymn Tune* were forging an American musical identity from folk elements and hymnody. Both composers found their way to Hollywood, and Copland's scores for *Of Mice and Men* (1940) and *Our Town* (1940), along with Thomson's for the documentaries *The Plow That Broke the Plains* (1936), *The River* (1937), and *Louisiana Story* (1948) were highly influential. Perhaps because the western as a genre focused so intently on American values, its scores have been especially shaped by this aesthetic such as Dimitri Tiomkin's for *Red River* (1948), Jerome Moross's for *The Big Country* (1958), and Elmer Bernstein's for *The Magnificent Seven* (1960). The prominent quotation of hymns, especially in the westerns of John Ford such as *My Darling Clementine* (1946) and *The Searchers* (1956), is another articulation of this musical aesthetic. Contemporary Hollywood films continue to rely on the harmonic textures and modal melodies of American folk song (and Copland's influence looms large) to encode Americanness in such scores as Randy Newman's for *The Natural* (1983) about the quintessentially American sport of baseball. Even a western steeped in a Modernist musical idiom (*There Will Be Blood*, 2007) cannot resist the inclusion of a hymn.

Like Copland and Thomson in the United States, the concert composer and conductor Silvestre Revueltas in Mexico evoked nationalism through the use of traditional music. But Revueltas put a Modernist spin on that music in *Let's Go with Pancho Villa!* (1936) and *The Night of the Mayas* (1939). Inspired by rather than quoting from indigenous musics and folk traditions, Revueltas refracted Mexico's distinctive folk melodies and instrumentations through Modernist techniques, finding a unique form of national musical expression. Revueltas himself can be glimpsed in *Let's Go with Pancho Villa!* where he can be seen playing the piano, and heard in the Hollywood film *Sin City* (2005) where his tone poem for orchestra, *Sensamaya*, is quoted at length.

In Hollywood, jazz infiltrated the film score in the 1950s and gravitated toward film noir, crime film, and urban melodramas in scores such as Alex North's for *A Streetcar Named Desire* (1951), Elmer Bernstein's for *Sweet Smell of Success* (1957) featuring the Chico Hamilton Quintet, John Lewis's for *Odds Against Tomorrow* (1959), featuring the Modern Jazz Quartet, and Henry Mancini's for *Touch of Evil* (1958). Jazz was initially associated with urban decadence, and the extent to which these associations cling to jazz is an open question among film scholars. Krin Gabbard, for instance, argues that Hollywood jazz scores continue to reveal ideologies of race, gender, and sexuality. More recently, Clint Eastwood (who also composes film scores) and Spike Lee have utilized jazz in *Bird* (1988) and *Mo' Better Blues* (1990) respectively. A number of prominent jazz artists in the United States have been tapped to score films: Duke Ellington for *Anatomy of a Murder* (1959), Charles Mingus for *Shadows* (1960), Herbie Hancock for *Death Wish* (1974), and Joshua Redmond for *Vanya on 42nd Street* (1994) among others. Miles Davis, whose music has been used in many films including *Groundhog Day* (1993) and *Pleasantville* (1998), scored only a few himself. In one, the French film *Elevator to the Gallows* (1958), Davis improvised the score. Although scores comprised entirely of jazz are not commonplace, "jazzy" melodies, instruments, and rhythms turn up in the musical vocabularies of many film composers. Jazz scores are heard all over the world such as Toshiro Mayazumi's for *When a Woman Ascends the Stairs* (1960).

The unconventional rhythms, intimate and unusual configurations of instruments, and the dissonant and sometimes atonal harmonies of Modernism were writ large in Leonard Rosenman's scores for *East of Eden* (1955) and *Rebel Without a Cause* (1955), Leonard Bernstein's for *On the Waterfront* (1954), and Alex North's for *Spartacus* (1960). But Modernism could also be heard, most potently, in a series of scores Bernard Herrmann composed for Alfred Hitchcock. These scores bear the imprint of Modernism: striking instrumentation such as the all-string ensemble for *Psycho* (1960) or the all-brass ensemble for the discarded *Torn Curtain* (1966) score; arresting rhythms such as the habanera from *Vertigo* (1958) or the fandango from *North by Northwest* (1950); dissonant harmonies—the shrieking violin glissandi in the shower scene from *Psycho*—and polytonality—the famous *Vertigo* chord—two perfectly conventional tonal chords, played simultaneously.

Serialism, often called twelve-tone music, would also make its mark in mid-century. Serialism is a method of composition associated with Arnold Schoenberg in which all twelve pitches in the Western scale are used equally to avoid establishing any tonality. Listen for it in Rosenman's score for *The Cobweb* (1955) as well as in Scott Bradley's scores for Tom and Jerry cartoons at MGM. Quipped Bradley, "I hope that Dr. Schoenberg will forgive me for using *his system* to produce funny music, but even the boys in the orchestra laughed when we were recording it."

Beginning in the 1960s, the influence of Minimalism could be heard in films. Avoiding emotional triggers, Minimalist scores gravitate instead to the structure of the film, deliberately leaving audiences to respond emotionally on their own. Characterized by repetitive musical figures, which disturb conventional notions of rhythm and time, Minimalism attracted widespread attention through Philip Glass's mesmeric scores for *Koyaanisqatsi* (1983) and *The Thin Blue Line* (1988) and more recently *The Hours* (2002) and *Cassandra's Dream* (2007). Michael Nyman's collaboration with Peter Greenaway also exploits the distinctive techniques of Minimalism, particularly in *The Draughtsman's Contract* (1982) where repetitive musical structures find their analogue in the narrative construction of the film.

Periodizing film history is never easy. Even the seemingly obvious divide between silent and sound production is not clean and neat. When it comes to film music, neither is the divide between the first half of the twentieth century and the second. Musical trends, such as the rise of Minimalism, which began in the first half of the century, find fruition in the second; composers such as Bernard Herrmann or the team of Shankar-Jaikashan, who begin careers on one side of the half-century mark end well on the other; film industries operating before 1960, such as the Egyptian, influence the development of film industries in other Arab countries operating after 1960; and major developments, such as the trajectory of the classical Hollywood film score or the influence of Modernism do not fall neatly either pre- or post-1960. And yet, breaking up such a large expanse of film music history as the one that spans the end of the 1920s through the first decade of the twenty-first century seems necessary to keep the material from becoming overwhelming. And so I have drawn a boundary here at a point somewhere in the 1960s and will pick up the story in the next chapter.

Chapter 6
A history of film music III: 1960–present

Film music was transformed in the late twentieth century. The diverse practices that developed for the use of song and background music began to meld in the compilation score, a formidable new model for the use of music in film. Popular music moved to the forefront, an "advance" that harkens back to the earliest days of silent film accompaniment. World music became increasingly audible, and globalization began to influence the funding, production, and distribution of films. As we enter the twenty-first century, these changes have had a powerful impact on film music.

In mid-century, film responded to a specific set of challenges: the rise of auteurist directors and the development of an international film community; the impact of experiments in film form and style; repressive political regimes, which limited artistic expression; diminishing audiences; and changing audience demographics.

New challenges, new practices

One response, in evidence in two of the world's largest film industries, Bollywood and Hollywood, was to update ongoing traditions. In Bollywood, new genres such as the action film and crime film, and new musical influences such as rock 'n' roll, disco, and rap were accommodated. Music director Rahul Dev ("R. D.")

Burman, for instance, mixed elements of disco and rock with the folk traditions of his native Bengal. Although film songs have never disappeared from Hindi cinema, their prevalence in these new genres diminished, their form was impacted by the influx of new and diverse musical influences, especially rock 'n' roll, and their performance began to be incorporated in a more naturalistic way.

Hollywood, too, had adopted new musical vocabularies and idioms, which by mid-century had largely displaced Romanticism. There were always big-budget films that clung to the older model such as *Lawrence of Arabia* (1962) and *Doctor Zhivago* (1963), with scores by Maurice Jarre. But the dramatic comeback of the Romantic idiom in a symphonic deployment would be staged in the late 1970s and early 1980s by John Williams with the phenomenal success of his scores for the *Star Wars* trilogy (1977–83). The romantic idiom and symphonic form remain an attractive option for big-budget, action-adventure blockbusters, such as *Out of Africa* (1985) and *Dances with Wolves* (1990) with scores by John Barry, and *The Lord of the Rings* trilogy (2001–03) scored by Howard Shore. New musical responses were also being forged, and it is to those that we now turn.

In the cinema of auteur directors and in the international film community where they circulated, Modernism became something of a mark of authenticity, a sign of the suspicion of and refusal to adopt normative filmic conventions that manipulate the viewer. Directors often labeled as Modernist, such as Michelangelo Antonioni, Ingmar Bergman, Luis Buñuel, Alain Resnais, Claude Chabrol, and Carlos Saura, fashioned films that used music very sparingly. Avoiding many of film music's traditional functions such as establishing mood and atmosphere and channeling emotion, composers for the films of these Modernist directors produced something akin to Brecht's noted distanciation effect with music devoid of emotional triggers for the audience. Hanns Eisler, in the score for Resnais's documentary *Night and Fog* (1955), undercut powerful images of Nazis on parade with unexpected pizzicato strings. Luis de Pablo, in the score for Saura's *The Garden of Delights* (1970), signaled a character's mental breakdown through *musique concrete,* an avant-garde practice using nonmusical sounds to make music. Alain Robbe-Grillet, who wrote the screenplay for Resnais's *Last Year at Marienbad* (1961), had wanted only noises captured on location for the accompaniment. That, however, is not what he got. Instead, the composer Francis Seyrig provided a fugue for organ and Romantically inflected orchestral music, creating a lush but disorienting effect given the sterility of the stiff, formally dressed characters and endless hallways.

The French New Wave is an excellent example of the ways in which unconventional choices found expression in the film score in the second half of the twentieth century. Directors such as François Truffaut, Chabrol, Jacques Rivette, Resnais, and especially Jean-Luc Godard sought iconoclastic scores for their fresh and often revolutionary approaches to film content, construction, and style. Chabrol and Truffaut established long-term collaborations with composers to give their films a distinctive sound (Pierre Jansen scored more than thirty films for Chabrol; Georges Delerue scored eleven for Truffaut), but perhaps the most striking examples of New Wave scores are those for several of Godard's films: Martial Solal's jazzy score for *Breathless* (1959); Michel Legrand's theme and variations for *Vivre sa vie* (1962), which abruptly and arbitrarily stop mid-phrase; Antoine Duhamel's score for *Weekend* (1967), which features a concert pianist in a barnyard, and Gabriel Yared's for *Sauve qui peut (la vie)* (1980), where characters in a shoot-out run past the musicians playing the score.

Using stylishly Modernist effects, such as Serialism and *musique concrete*, combined with elements of popular music, folk influences, Celtic song, Gregorian chant, mariachi trumpets, and an ensemble of players the size of a symphony orchestra, Ennio Morricone created a series of memorable scores for Sergio Leone's spaghetti westerns of the 1960s. In *The Good, The Bad, and The*

Ugly (1966), Morricone uses conventional melody played on an electric guitar, an ocarina (an ancient flute), and a harmonica, along with much more unconventional types of scoring including whistling, yodeling, grunting, vocalizations at times unrecognizable as human, whipcracks, and gunshots. Morricone turned his back on the Hollywood conventions for western film scores that emphasized the melodic contours and harmonic textures of folk song and hymnody. In the process, Morricone provided a new model for the western film score. The Hollywood western *3:10 to Yuma* (2007) is an example of Morricone's continuing legacy to the genre.

The German New Wave also uses music unconventionally, gravitating toward pastiche in its scores, which quote everything from Bach to the Beatles. Music calls attention to itself, performed in exaggerated, skewed, or clichéd ways, or yanked out of context into startling relationships with the images. Caryl Flinn argues that these disquieting relationships call authenticity itself into question and force viewers into critical awareness of the issues of history, memory, and identity tied up with Germany's past. Per Raben, who composed a series of scores for Rainer Werner Fassbinder (and helped choose the preexisting songs), echoes earlier Modernists in using music to shock. In *The Marriage of Maria Braun* (1979), Raben arranges a Nazi soldier's song for xylophone and glockenspiel, deliberately invoking childhood and innocence. In *Chinese Roulette* (1976), Raben uses dance forms to accompany a character who cannot walk without crutches. For a series of films by Werner Herzog, the music group Popol Vuh (named after a Mayan book of mythology) created a series of arresting cues, many generated electronically and some using native instruments, which obscured precise ethnic origin—the quasi-religious Buddhist chanting (by the Bavarian State Opera chorus) in *Aguirre: The Wrath of God* (1972), set in the Amazon rain forest during the Spanish conquest of the New World, or the quasi-Gregorian chanting, accompanied by a sitar, in *Nosferatu* (1979), Herzog's remake of F. W. Murnau's 1922 vampire film.

In Japan in the 1960s, Tôru Takemitsu created innovative scores for a number of films successful internationally. Takemitsu, who was the leading composer of art music in Japan, had developed a style fusing musical elements of East and West, which proved accessible to the international art-house audience. Nevertheless, many of his scores are highly experimental and bring an unexpected edge to what listeners expect to hear (or not hear). In *Kwaidan* (1964) Takemitsu used *musique concrete* to great effect in the representation of ghostly presences; in *Woman of the Dunes* (1964) he electronically manipulated the recording process to create a dreamlike wash of sound. Takemitsu's film work is also marked by a distinctive placement of both sound and silence, and he is sometimes credited with the sound design as well as the score. In Kurosawa's *Ran* (1985), sound disappears in the graphically violent battle sequence, replaced by an extended symphonic cue. The disturbing contrast between the beautiful, elegiac melody and the scene of slaughter is abruptly halted when a gunshot is heard. The music disappears at this point, and the soundtrack is filled with the grotesque sounds of death. Explains Takemitsu, "I want to give sounds the freedom to breathe."

In the 1950s Indian directors, working outside the Hindi industry, reached out to the new international audience. One of them, Satyajit Ray, working in the Bengali industry centered in Calcutta (now Kolkata), quickly established himself as one of the new auteurs. To a much greater extent than Hindi cinema, Bengali cinema depended upon Western musics including US pop music, Latin American music, Iberian music, Western art music, and Hollywood scoring techniques. Further, music was used more conventionally in Bengali cinema than in Hindi cinema, with musical performances either eliminated altogether or more narratively justified and relegated to naturalistic settings as nightclubs, parties, or dream sequences. Ray claimed, "If I were asked to find room for six songs in a story that is not expressly a 'musical,' I would have to throw up my hands and give up."

Electronic music

Electronic music was initially confined to horror films and science fiction. But it got its start in Miklós Rózsa's scores for *Spellbound* and *The Lost Weekend* (both 1945). which featured the eerie-sound of the theremin, an electronic instrument "played" by the movement of the performer's hands through radio waves. Akira Ifukube used electronic sound produced by a tape recorder in his score for *Godzilla* (1956), and in the same year Louis and Bebe Barron introduced the first completely electronically produced score, *Forbidden Planet* (1956). Electronic music moved into the mainstream and high visibility with Giorgio Moroder's synthesized score for *Midnight Express* (1978) and Vangelis's for *Chariots of Fire* (1981) and *Bladerunner* (1982). The synthesizer can reproduce the sound of acoustic instruments through sampling, a kind of digital picture of a sound, which can then be manipulated. With the advent in 1983 of MIDI (Musical Instrument Digital Interface), digital language was standardized, and electronic instruments and computers could be synchronized. In other words, they could communicate with one another. For economic reasons, the synthesizer has often replaced acoustic instruments, and it displaced many studio musicians when it was first introduced in the 1980s.

The synthesizer has also made the sounds of instruments from all parts of the world more accessible. Gabriel Yared's score for *The English Patient* (1996), for example, uses a traditional symphony orchestra along with the synthesized sound of the *quanoun*, a traditional Middle Eastern stringed instrument. For *Malevil* (1980), Yared created the score from the synthesized sounds of nature, his own voice, the quanoun, and the oud, another traditional Middle Eastern instrument and an ancestor of the lute. The synthesizer has also allowed artists, not trained as composers, to create film scores, such as the director John

Carpenter, whose own synthesized music can be heard in many of his films, including *Assault on Precinct 13* (1976), *Halloween* (1978) and *Escape from New York* (1981).

The most innovative use of the synthesizer has been to create sounds that a traditional orchestra cannot make. Many composers have experimented with its capabilities: David Shire uses the distorted sound of a synthesized piano in *The Conversation* (1974) to suggest the protagonist's mental instability. Quincy Jones synthesizes sounds of electronic wiretapping and mixes them with a jazz combo in the score for *The Anderson Tapes* (1971). Cliff Martinez uses a synthesizer to create a kind of musical ambient sound throughout *Traffic* (2000) and to produce an otherworldly effect for the last scene of the film (a baseball game). In many film industries throughout the world, synthesized scores have become the norm.

Ray's Apu trilogy, among his earliest films, was scored by Ravi Shankar. Shankar had traveled extensively in the West but used exclusively Indian instruments and classical and folk music traditions for his film scores, apparently to Ray's dismay. Ray would soon begin composing himself. Nevertheless, some of the most profoundly moving moments in Ray's oeuvre occur in Shankar's scores: in *Pather Panchali* (1955), when a returning father is told by his wife that their daughter has died, and the sound of their dialogue is replaced by the wail of the high-pitched tar *shehnai*, or in *Aparajito* (1956), when Apu's mother slaps Apu in the face, and their mutual shock is registered after the fact by percussion.

In Latin America, the film industries of Mexico, Brazil, and Argentina faced stiff competition in the second half of the twentieth century from cheap and accessible Hollywood imports.

6. Ravi Shankar scored a series of films for the director Satyajit Ray in the 1950s, utilizing many native Indian instruments, including the sitar.

Filmmakers found themselves caught between the demands of commercial success (and the pressure to emulate Hollywood models) and the commitment to the social role of cinema as an expression of uniquely national concerns. Many filmmakers, especially those with newfound status as international auteurs tried to do both as the scores for their films attest, combining elements of Hollywood scoring, European art music, and indigenous music. Even avowedly political filmmakers found themselves in this mediated musical space. The scores for the documentaries of the Brazilian filmmaker Glauber Rocha, in films such as *Barravento* (1962), *Black God, White Devil* (1964) and *Land in August* (1967), include originally composed musical cues along with quotations from European art music (Bach, Verdi), Brazilian art music (Heitor Villa-Lobos, himself an intersection of European and Brazilian influences), and Brazilian and Afro-Brazilian musics (the samba and the candomblé). In Paul Leduc's *Frida: naturaleza viva* (1984), Mexican *corridos*, Spanish *zarzuela*, and European art music (Saint-Saëns, Sibelius, Prokofiev) blend. The score for Fernando Meirelles's *City of God* (2002) by Antonio Pinto and Ed Cortes mixes original composition with idioms popular in the United States such as rap, soul, disco, and Brazilian samba, and through this juxtaposition raises questions about the ability of Brazilian indigenous music to compete with the global reach of pop music. One particularly interesting example is Argentinean director Fernando Solanas's *Tangos! The Exile of Gardel* (1985) with tangos by noted composer Astor Piazzolla, the founder of *nuevo tango*, an infusion of tango, jazz, and European art music. Solanas wrote the lyrics himself. Playing off the popular cinematic tradition of the *tanguedia* and speaking to national issues (the military junta that ruled from 1976 to 1983 had banned tangos in order to destroy allegiance to Argentinean culture), the use of tangos positions the film in an intriguing nexus of escapist musicals and trenchant political commentary. In Spain, the early films of Pedro Almodóvar had a similar musical profile, exploiting indigenous traditional and popular Spanish musics, such as the bolero, for nationalistic purpose.

In the Egyptian film industry, filmmakers also faced commercial pressures. As popular music in Egypt has become more international, so too have the scores for commercial Egyptian cinema. Some filmmakers have continued to explore the traditions of traditional Arab music, both traditional and contemporary. Lebanese singer Magda al-Rumi can be heard in Youssef Chahine's *The Return of the Prodigal Son* (1976), and performances of Arab song are interpolated into both Khairy Beshara's *The Crabs* (1991) and Daoud Abd El-Sayyed's *al-Kitkat* (1991). Pop singer Muhammad Munir is heard in Beshara's *Necklace and Bracelet* (1986); and the pop stars Amr Diyab and Muhammad Fu-ad in Beshara's *Ice Cream in Glin* (1993) and *Abracadabra America* (1993). Assia Djebar's *The Nuba of the Women of Mont Chenoua* (1976) features nuba, traditional music originating in Arab Spain in the Middle Ages, as both the subject and score.

Elsewhere, other kinds of challenges were caused by political regimes that repressed artistic expression. By the 1950s many of the most renowned Soviet composers eagerly pursued film work, having seen their concert works banned due to charges of Formalism (using Modernist techniques, which, it was alleged, rendered their music inaccessible to the masses). Shostakovich, Khachaturian, Shebalin, and Prokofiev all turned to film scoring at some point in their careers: they found that being out of the spotlight had its rewards. Many of these composers recycled music in their film scores that would not have been acceptable for the Soviet concert hall. Party officials seemed not to notice. During some of the worst moments of political repression, some films dispensed with music altogether. Yet Shostakovich managed a long career in film, collaborating with Gregori Kozintsev from *The New Babylon* (1929) to *King Lear* (1971) and (carefully) using Modernist effects. In the 1970s, when limitations on artistic expression began to be lifted, Soviet directors such as Andrei Tarkovsky began to reach international audiences. Even rock 'n' roll appeared in Soviet films by the 1980s.

The Islamic Revolution dealt a near-fatal blow to the Iranian film industry in 1979, although the industry had struggled in the 1950s and 1960s against competition from Indian and Hollywood film industries. In the long run, however, the new government ended up largely supporting what had become known as Iranian New Wave cinema. The Middle Eastern scholar Hamid Naficy argues that official government condemnation of the West combined with strict censorship actually fostered an environment in which a uniquely Iranian cinema could be reborn. (It should be noted, however, that some Iranian films that reached the international art-house circuit were banned internally.) Cinema became the most popular form of entertainment in Iran in the 1980s. Iran's vibrant musical scene, disrupted by the Revolution, found its way into film as many prominent concert hall composers moved to film scoring, which both provided a livelihood and access to audiences through popular recordings of film scores.

The scores reflect this refocus on national issues. Although many New Wave Iranian films hew to a neo-realist aesthetic and use music very sparingly, some prominently feature music. Hossein Alizadeh, a classically trained conductor and composer, used elements of traditional Iranian music in a series of films for director Bahman Ghobadi including *Half Moon* (2006) and *Turtles Can Fly* (2004). *Half Moon* concerns a family of musicians, Kurdish exiles in Iran, who return to Iraqi Kurdistan after the fall of Saddam Hussein to perform in a celebratory concert. The story provides plenty of opportunities for performances of indigenous music, and the score features Persian instruments, some of which are viewed being made in the film. In Mohsen Makhmalbaf's *Gabbeh* (1996), Alizadeh's score gravitates to the otherworldly aspects of the narrative (the story concerns a love story told from the perspective of woman whose spirit lives in a *gabbeh* or Persian carpet), which are represented musically by unusual combinations of Persian and Western instruments.

The Communist takeover of China in 1949 ushered in an era of state-financed and controlled cinema, not unlike that under Joseph Stalin in the Soviet Union. After the vitality of the early sound-era scores, those in the first years of the People's Republic of China often seem conventional by comparison, with music used to supply mood and atmosphere. Production in the PRC slowed and by the 1970s had virtually ceased; the action had moved to Hong Kong, which would become the most prolific of the Chinese-language film industries. A low point came with Mao Tse-tung's Cultural Revolution, 1976–86, when traditional Chinese music and Western music of any kind were banned.

It would take until the Open Door Policy of the 1980s for the Chinese film industry to recover and enter the international film community with a new generation of filmmakers, dubbed the Fifth Generation, and a new breed of composers, the New Wave, leading the way. They were, however, not immune to internal censorship, and many films that had left a large footprint internationally were not seen in the PRC. New Wave composers rose to prominence scoring these films. Many had studied in the West. Zhao Jiping is the most prominent among them scoring several films for Zhang Yimou—*Red Sorghum* (1987), *Ju Dou* (1990), and *Raise the Red Lantern* (1991) and for Chen Kaige—*Yellow Earth* (1984) and *Farewell My Concubine* (1993)—combining elements of traditional Chinese music with Western harmonies and instrumentation. For *Farewell My Concubine*, Zhao exploited Chinese opera and achieved some intriguing effects using its percussive instruments, which he electronically altered. Zhao's scores have not always garnered critical kudos. Mervyn Cooke writes of Zhao's score for *Red Firecracker, Green Firecracker* (1994): it "is remarkably close to how one might imagine Vaughn Williams arranging Asian folk material."

The most internationally successful Chinese composer, however, is Tan Dun, who found himself reassigned from music school in Beijing to a rice paddy in Hunan for two years during the Cultural Revolution. Nonetheless, it is precisely Chinese and Asian musical elements with Western forms and instrumentation, those that were banned during the revolution, that Tan Dun has utilized in his career in the concert hall as well as in film. An Oscar-winner for his score for Ang Lee's *Crouching Tiger, Hidden Dragon* (2000), a U.S./Taiwan co-production, Tan combined ancient Chinese instruments, Chinese opera, Japanese kabuki musical

7. Tan Dun (*left*) won an Oscar in 2000 (Best Original Score) for his score for *Crouching Tiger, Hidden Dragon*, which prominently features solos by the cellist Yo-Yo Ma.

traditions, a battery of Asian percussion, and a Western symphony orchestra with the world-famous cellist Yo-Yo Ma. Like Zhao Jiping, Tan Dun has experienced his share of criticism for banking on Western fantasies of China. As he explains it, however, he is promoting Chinese music as part of the international language of music: "I'm Marco Polo going backward from East to West."

Indigenous music, both operatic and popular, continued to provide a crucial component in the development of Chinese-language film industries outside the PRC. In Hong Kong, in the Cantonese industry, films featuring Chinese opera continued as dependable audience pleasers well into the 1970s, and in the Mandarin industry, musicals tapped into indigenous popular music and dance. In Taiwan in the 1980s, the director Hou Hsiao-hsien began his career in a similar vein with a series of musicals starring pop singers Feng Feifei and Kenny Bee, and featuring numerous pop songs. Contemporary Hong Kong films continue to tap into a vibrant pop music aesthetic, featuring recording stars in acting roles and loading films with contemporary songs. Even John Woo's police thriller, *The Killer* (1989), has three songs performed by Sally Yeh, who plays the film's female lead.

The compilation film score

Popular music became a defining characteristic of film music in the second half of the twentieth century. As we have seen, national cinemas around the world, in countries as diverse as Egypt, Iran, India, the Soviet Union, China, Hong Kong, and Taiwan, had long been incorporating large amounts of popular music, foregrounded as performance or utilized in the background score and sometimes crossing the boundary between the two. By the 1960s popular songs had exploded onto the soundtrack in Hollywood, too. To some extent, Hollywood had always banked on popular songs, exploiting them in musicals, interpolating them into a variety of films, such as the memorable use of "As Time Goes By" in *Casablanca* (1942), or creating them from themes in the background score that caught the public's attention, such as Tara's theme in *Gone With the Wind* (1939). But in terms of the large-scale exploitation of popular music in the film score, Hollywood was a bit of a johnny-come-lately. In the 1950s, popular songs were being written expressly for use in the background score, such as Dimitri Tiomkin and Ned Washington's "Do Not Forsake Me Oh My Darling," for *High Noon* (1952). But it was the 1960s that saw the proliferation of popular song in the background score. *Breakfast at Tiffany's* (1961) played no small part in this development. Henry Mancini's "Moon River" was performed by Audrey Hepburn in the film and threaded instrumentally through the background score. "Moon River" won the Academy Award for "Best Song" and a Grammy for "Song of the Year" in 1961. The soundtrack album was on Billboard's charts for more than ninety-six weeks.

Hollywood's attraction to popular music is understandable, given the commercial pressures it faced mid-century. Viewership was getting younger; television was siphoning off audiences; the studio system was reeling from a series of legal actions dismantling the vertical integration of production, distribution, and exhibition; and the growth of pop music expanded exponentially in the 1950s and 1960s. Hollywood as an institutional practice was breaking apart, and it responded with diversification, acquiring, among other things, record companies to cross-promote studios' products (and record companies began acquiring film studios). Jeff Smith argues persuasively that in practice, popular song was adapted to the principles of classical Hollywood scoring and was used to respond to the dramatic needs of the narrative and to control emotional response. Think of the use of the song "My Heart Will Go On" in *Titanic* (1997), sung by Céline Dion in the end credits but first heard throughout the film in different arrangements and instrumentations as the love theme for the two protagonists.

But the widespread use of popular song did shift Hollywood's musical idiom to a more contemporary and popular reference point; it soon became a virtual requirement to include a pop song, which could add to a film's profitability. Indeed, the inclusion of a pop song, often in the end credits, has accelerated to such a point that not even a fantasy epic set in a mythological time period, such *The Lord of the Rings*, is free of them.

But it was rock 'n' roll that would prove the most important new form of popular music in the second half of the twentieth century. First heard briefly in *The Blackboard Jungle* (1955), where Bill Haley and the Comets performed "Rock Around the Clock" for the opening credits, rock 'n' roll was initially exploited to target young viewers. Rock soon infiltrated the background score in films like *Shaft* (1971) scored by Isaac Hayes, and *Sorcerer* (1977) and *Risky Business* (1983) scored by Tangerine Dream. Rock would also prove a fertile seedbed for a new generation of film composers: Peter Gabriel of Genesis, Mark Knopfler of Dire Straits, Danny Elfman of Oingo Boingo, and Ryuichi Sakamoto of the Yellow Magic Orchestra, among many others. But there was an even more radical model waiting in the wings that would utilize rock 'n' roll in new and transformative ways.

That new model that emerged in the second half of the twentieth century not only accommodated popular music, it challenged conventional scoring practices that privileged original composition. The compilation score, as it has come to be known, developed in the 1960s and 1970s and bears more than a passing resemblance to earlier bricolage models in China, Iran, and Egypt, the pastiche model of New German Cinema, and the use of song in Bollywood. Compilation scores consist of a series of songs, usually preexisting, sometimes emanating from a source within the film but more often used as background music. These discreet musical pieces are largely derived from noncinematic sources (for example, opera, art music, but most frequently popular music and especially rock 'n' roll), often used in their original recorded format, and sometimes supplemented by original songs and orchestral scoring. The Beatles' phenomenally successful and highly influential films *A Hard Day's Night* (1964) and *Help!* (1965) are two early examples.

Songs are different from instrumental music in several ways. Songs can draws an audience's conscious attention more directly than background music and thus establish meaning more quickly and efficiently; songs have access to language, specifically lyrics, which can be a very explicit means of transmitting meaning. On the other hand, songs have a structure of their own and may not be as flexible as music composed expressly for the film. Because preexisting songs are more immediately recognizable, they also trail with them personal histories and trigger memories, experiences, and emotions, which may be at odds with the film's dramatic needs. Still, songs are constituted through the language of music; they utilize many of the same musical elements as the background score and often fulfill similar functions: providing unity, creating mood, heightening atmosphere, aiding characterization, establishing geographic space and time period, and connecting an audience emotionally to a film.

Anahid Kassabian argues that the compilation score opens up new types of identification processes for audiences. She views the increased emphasis on song, especially in contemporary Hollywood film, as a positive and even liberating development. For Kassabian, the compilation score provides new possibilities for audiences to forge individual relationships to films and creates space for alternative voices, especially those of women and minorities, to be heard. Think of the ways in which the recordings of female singers in *Thelma and Louise* (1991) give privileged insight into the protagonists' inner lives: Martha Reeves singing "Wild Night" or Tammy Wynette, "I Don't Wanna Play House."

Compilation scores have dramatically changed the landscape of film scoring. Responsibility shifts from the composer to the director or the music supervisor, or both. Choosing music generally precedes the shooting; directors want to know which songs are being used and the process of clearing copyright on songs is a time-consuming process.

Compilation scores are often characterized by their eclecticism. Consider Wong Kar-wai's *Chungking Express* (1994), which includes Faye Wong's covers of "Dreams" by the Cranberries and "Bluebeard" by the Cocteau Twins; Dinah Washington's "What a Difference A Day Makes"; Dennis Brown's "Things in Life"; The Mamas and the Papas' "California Dreamin'"; and an original song, "Baraque," by Michael Galasso. The kaleidoscopic compilation score for Alfonso Cuarón's *Y tu mamá también* (2001) is comprised entirely of source music and includes dozens of recordings by English and Spanish language performers: rockers Frank Zappa of the United States and Brian Eno of Britain, Australian singer Natalie Imbruglia, Spanish rap star La Mala (Rodriguez), the psychedelic 1970s Mexican rock band La Revolucion de Emiliano Zapata, Mexican pop singer Edith Marquez, alternative Mexican rockers Café Tacuba, and legendary Sonoran guitarist and composer Ignacio Penunuri Jaime.

World music

World music has become an increasingly high-profile component of film scoring, both in the compilation score, where it is quoted, and in the originally composed score, where its instrumentations are borrowed. In use since ca. 1980s, the term "world music" is a fairly diffuse and loosely defined concept; it generally refers to non-Western, indigenous popular music marketed to an international audience. World music has turned up in many compilation scores: *qawwali*, Sufi Muslim devotional music originating in northern India, sung by the noted Pakistani singer Nusrat Fateh Ali Khan in *The Last Temptation of Christ* (1988) and *Dead Man Walking* (1995); North African *raï*, itself a veritable melting pot of worldwide influences, sung by *raï* star Khaled, in *The Fifth Element* (1997)—and in original scores such as *The Ice Storm* (1997) where Mychael Danna employs a Native American flute and Sudanese gamelans. It remains an open question whether world music in a film's soundtrack is a positive development, introducing audiences to music previously unavailable to them or a negative one, an exploitation and commodification of world music and yet another example of the West's co-opting of non-Western cultures for commercial gain. Perhaps it is both.

Film has, in some sense, always been a global enterprise. While many films are tied to their countries of origin by their sources of funding and their audiences (although even this is becoming less and less true), they have long been infused with global influences. That trail of globalization can be followed through the history of film music. The influx of composers from one country and culture to another, and the diffusion of the musical practices they bring with them is a process that began long before the concept of globalization came into focus. Film music has always been transnational: European composers emigrating to Hollywood trailing Romanticism with them; early sound film scores in China quoting Strauss waltzes as well as leftist revolutionary songs; production numbers in Egyptian films drawing from Latin American and African musical elements; *Film Farsi* exploiting cues from Hollywood films alongside Persian music played on traditional Persian instruments; Hindi filmmaking influencing Hollywood film scores today. In fact, global musical influences routinely turn up in Hollywood and in some surprising places: the *duduk*, an Armenian wind instrument, can be heard in Hans Zimmer and Lisa Gerrard's score for *Gladiator* (2000).

The compilation score, too, has taken on a decidedly global cast: classic US and British rock along with classical and contemporary Mexican music in *Y tu mamá también*; contemporary Hong Kong punk rock alongside quotes from classical Hollywood film scores in *Kill Bill*, Vols. 1 and 2 (2003–04); US pop, reggae, and Cantonese covers of rock songs in *Chungking Express*, a Chinese-language film made in Hong Kong by a director born in mainland China. Film composers themselves cross national borders in their identity. Consider Gabriel Yared who was born and raised in Lebanon, immigrated to France, then Brazil, back to France, and then London where he scores Hollywood films. Scores are often produced globally now. In order to create *Crouching Tiger, Hidden Dragon*, cellist Yo-Yo Ma, supervised by Tan Dun and Ang Lee, recorded his solos in New York, which were later integrated with the orchestral score recorded in Shanghai with Tan conducting a Western symphony with traditional Chinese instruments and a battery of Asian percussion.

A composer who encompasses the global cast of film music in the twenty-first century is Alberto Iglesias, a Spaniard, whose twentieth-century scores, especially for the films of Pedro Almodóvar, included a wide range of musical traditions including tango, folk, jazz, and classical Hollywood film scoring. In 2007, Iglesias created a sarangi-infused score for *The Kite Runner*, using Middle Eastern instruments such as the *bansuri* and the *ney*, wooden flutes, the *santur*, a dulcimer, the *rubab*, an Afghani lute, and the tabla. "To make film music," he claims, "one needs to rely on that global comprehension but one can also change, invert, and modify."

Chapter 7
Composers and their craft

This chapter is devoted to film composers, those men and women who compose the score, the original music we hear in the background of a film. Although songwriters compose the songs heard in films, and music supervisors help to choose and compile preexisting music, film composers work quite differently. Here I would like to put the spotlight on the composers of some of the most memorable and highly recognizable music in the twentieth century, originally composed film scores.

Where do film composers come from? How do composers work when they are scoring a film? What is the process and how does it differ from one institutional practice to another, from one national cinema to another, and from one era to another? What are the basic issues involved in scoring all films? What are the key relationships among the various personnel who collaborate on a film, and where does the composer fit into this framework? Which composers have managed to forge collaborative partnerships with directors? Which composers have been able to wield power in the institutional settings in which they work? This chapter sketches out some answers to these questions and gives readers a fuller picture of some of the personalities and processes that characterize film composers and their craft.

Film composers hail from all walks of musical life: the concert hall—Dmitri Shostakovich, Sergei Prokofiev, Aaron Copland, Ralph Vaughn Williams, Tôru Takemitsu, Tan Dun, Philip Glass, and John Corigliano; the opera house—Erich Wolfgang Korngold and Richard Hageman; Broadway—Max Steiner and Alfred Newman; performance careers—Ravi Shankar, Victor Young, and Miles Davis; television—Henry Mancini and Quincy Jones; advertising—A. R. Rahman; and rock music—Peter Gabriel, Danny Elfman, Ryuichi Sakamoto, Jonny Greenwood, and the groups Pink Floyd, Tangerine Dream, and Popol Vuh. Film composing can comprise a career, or it can be part of a diverse musical life, which includes all of the above. Composers have complained, sometimes bitterly, about the constraints of scoring film; others have found it liberating and often rework their film music for the concert hall (Takemitsu, who recycled film music for the concert hall) or vice versa (Greenwood, who recycled concert hall music for film); and for some, film composing may even have saved their lives (Korngold, Prokofiev, Shostakovich).

The process of composing a film score depends upon a number of factors: institutional practices and the circulation of power within them (large studio systems like Hollywood, where composers are part of an assembly-line mode of production, versus Bollywood, where music directors developed considerable freedom in the production of the score, and many enjoy celebrity status); the relationships at work on a given film (longtime collaborations between directors and composers, for example, Steven Spielberg and John Williams, or Rainer Werner Fassbinder and Per Raben); the power of the director and his or her interest in determining the musical score (Akira Kurosawa, John Ford, Jean-Luc Godard, and Wong Kar-wai are just a few directors who have had an active hand in shaping scores for their films); and the individual personalities and proclivities of the composers themselves (such as the notoriously prickly Bernard Herrmann who insisted, "I have the final say about my music; otherwise I refuse to do the music for the film").

Core issues in composing for films

There is a core set of issues that film composers around the world address. Although composers can work through these issues in very different ways, the issues themselves are surprisingly similar. Where and when to begin the process of composition is among the first of them. Some composers prefer to read the script for inspiration. Gabriel Yared, for one, will not take on a project without seeing the script. In his collaborations with Jean-Jacques Beineix, Yared read and discussed the scripts with Beineix and met with the actors in preproduction. Yared's scores were largely complete before filming began so that Beineix could play Yared's music on the set. Takemitsu would read a script before taking a job and wanted to be brought into the production as early as possible, often visiting the set during filming. Elfman likes to visit the set during production, too, and has credited the sight of the *Batman* (1989) set as the inspiration for the score's theme. Liu Zhuang likes to read the script and go on location to get a feel for the material. For Ling Zifeng's *Border Town* (1984), she visited West Hunan and researched local folk music, which she was able to incorporate into the score. And Tan Dun claims that he and Ang Lee began their discussions about the score for *Crouching Tiger, Hidden Dragon* (2000) four years before production began.

These are exceptional experiences, however. Standard operating procedure in Hollywood and in the international film community in general is to bring the composer in after the film has been shot. (Animation often works in the reverse: composers create the score before animators begin their work, allowing intricate effects in the coordination of music and image.) Many composers prefer it this way. Steiner quipped: "I never read a script. I run a mile when I see one." Herrmann claimed that he "could never work from a script when scoring a Hitchcock film.... You can't guess his musical requirements ahead of time." Even Liu Zhuang waited until the editing was complete to begin the actual scoring: "But you know, even though a script [says] there should be music here or here or here, that always changes as the film is in progress." And as Maurice Jarre found out the hard way, composing ahead of time doesn't always work out. Jarre completed his score for *The Mosquito Coast* (1986) in advance of production so that director Peter Weir could play it on the set. And Weir did play Jarre's score during shooting; it was just not the one ultimately heard in the completed film. As Jarre explains it, Weir's conception of the music changed dramatically during filming, and Jarre, unable to recycle any of the precomposed material, had to compose an entirely new score for the release version.

Most composers will see the film for the first time in rough cut, an initial and provisional edit of the film. This allows composers to respond to what actually ends up on film but also puts them under tremendous time constraints. In the classical Hollywood studio system, composers were given a window of roughly three to six weeks, although certain composers, such as Korngold, had the prestige and thus the power to demand more time. That time frame has not changed substantially. Morricone, one of the world's most sought-after film composers, generally asks for one month. A. R. Rahman finished the score for *Slumdog Millionaire* (2008) in three weeks. The eight months that Yared had to compose the score for *Possession* (2002) was possible only because Yared scored the film before he had the opportunity to see any of it.

For most composers, scoring begins with spotting the film, that is screening the rough cut and deciding which spots need music and how much. Says John Barry, "The choices about where the music goes in a movie are the most important decisions you can make." He adds: "90 percent of the time those choices are really very clear and both the director and yourself are in sync." In general the task of spotting falls to the director, composer, and music editor who make these determinations depending upon the power of the director (or the extent to which he or she is invested in the score), the composer's ability to register his or her choices (as Morricone so delicately puts it, "sometimes...the director tends to assert himself…to the detriment of the authority of the composer"), and the nature of the relationships among the participants.

Some directors spot the films themselves and many with considerable skill. On *Slumdog Millionaire*, Danny Boyle spotted the film, and Rahman would email him four or five different musical options for each cue so that Boyle could decide on the one he liked. For Rahman, used to working in Bollywood where the music director's assistants "mark" the film (and the composer is in control), "[i]t was a totally different way of working." Still, says Rahman, who won two Oscars for the film, "it worked out all right."

Today, in the West and in many parts of the world, the director is a key figure in the creation of an original score; it is often his or her vision that the composer works to realize. This is not always easy, especially when directors, who tend to be visually oriented, try to communicate in musical terms. In a great collaboration, it somehow works out. Says Kevin Costner of working with John Barry on *Dances With Wolves* (1990): "We're not exactly sharing the same vocabulary…[but] he understands exactly what I mean." Sometimes the collaboration goes smoothly. Says Barry of working with Costner: "This was Kevin's first directorial job and he asked a lot of questions, and I explained why I was doing this and why I was doing that and I think for the most part it was very easy going."

Sometimes it doesn't go smoothly. When it does work, however, a composer's input can be revelatory. Paul Thomas Anderson, referring to *There Will Be Blood* (2007) says, "To make a film, the final big collaborator that you have is the composer. Jonny [Greenwood] was really one of the first people to see the film. And when he came back with a bunch of music, it actually helped show me what his impression of the film was. Which was terrific, because *I* had no impression."

Some institutional practices, such as the Hollywood studio system in its heyday, curtailed the power of the director in the chain of

8. Composer John Barry (*right*) and director Kevin Costner (*middle*) at a scoring session for *Dances with Wolves* (1990).

command. Responsibility for the score could be influenced by the film's producer, the head of the studio's music department, or even the studio chief. Until 1937, the head of the studio's music department, not the composer, collected the Oscar. Stories of musical ignorance on the part of Hollywood producers are legendary: the producer who wanted to "Frenchify" the score by adding French horns, or the producer who wanted the score to sound like Brahms and wanted to fly Brahms out to Hollywood to conduct it. Then there was the producer who wanted a Russian sound. When the score was played for him, although backwards, he was delighted with the result. David Raksin tells the story of a producer who claimed to love Alban Berg's *Wozzeck* and wanted the score to sound just like it. When Raksin put *Wozzeck* on the phonograph, the producer asked what crap he was playing. Miklós Rózsa remembers a producer who decreed that "the heroine's music was to be in a major key, the hero's in a minor key, and that when the two were together, the music should be both major and minor." Presumably the producer was not referring to polytonality.

Hollywood producers, however, did not have an exclusive on musical ignorance. Shankar Indorkar relates this experience in a recording studio in Bollywood: "So, some song we were playing...was in two flats, but it was too high for the singer. So [the arranger] said, 'We need to go a half tone lower,' so the music director, who knew that we were playing in two flats said, 'Okay, add one more flat.'"

Some producers and many studio chiefs wielded tremendous power in the Hollywood studio system. (And to this day, the studio, not the composer, owns any music created for its films.) Darryl F. Zanuck at Twentieth Century-Fox ordered new music composed and added to John Ford's *My Darling Clementine* (1946) after the preview. David O. Selznick's famous lengthy memos contained intricate notes on music that composers were expected to follow. It was to Selznick that composer Franz Waxman wrote when he had questions about the music for Hitchcock's *Rebecca* (1940) and Selznick who added additional music cues by Steiner to the score. Rózsa, describing his experience on *Spellbound* (1945), asserts that he saw Hitchcock only twice, complaining that he was "bombarded by the famous Selznick memos, which virtually told him how to compose and orchestrate the music scene by scene." Rózsa could be touchy about the director's input, contending that if directors had valuable input, he was willing to listen to them, but "if they were stupid, I refused them." John Corigliano, who left the concert hall for the screening room to score a handful of films, acknowledges that a film composer is an "employee." And for him, that is the most difficult part: "you have a job to do, and you have to please someone. On the other hand, you also have to please yourself. And that's the balance you try to maintain as a film composer—to please yourself and still satisfy the director and the producers."

But it is not only the Hollywood studio system that limits the power of the composer. Certain film industries have developed music formulas integral to success. Hindi cinema, *Film Farsi*,

Hong Kong cinema, Egyptian cinema, and Nigerian cinema require certain kinds and amounts of music. *Munna* (1954), the first Hindi film without song and dance, failed at the box office. It may be difficult if not impossible for composers to circumvent these expectations. And commercial pressures to include a pop song to appeal to certain audience demographics and to sell the score as a soundtrack album can be more powerful determinants than the studio chiefs of yore. Morricone describes being "pressed" to produce a score "as appealing as possible—melodic, easy, so that the majority of the audience likes it."

Collaboration

Nevertheless, throughout film history, certain directors have had a crucial relationship to the film scores for their films. Some have actually composed them. D. W. Griffith collaborated with Carl Breil on the score for his *The Birth of a Nation* (1915), supposedly composing its love theme. Teinosuki Kinugasa, who directed the avant-garde silent classic *A Page of Madness* (1927), composed the score himself when the film was rediscovered and reissued in the 1970s. Other directors who have turned their hand to composing include Charlie Chaplin (who depended upon orchestrators and arrangers to bring his musical ideas to fruition), John Carpenter, and Clint Eastwood.

Satyajit Ray is probably the director with the most extensive resume of film scores, composing many for his own films and several for other directors. Ray's relationships with the composers of his earliest films, Ravi Shankar, Ali Akbar Khan, and Ustad Vilayat Khan, were strained at best and Shankar, in particular, bristled at what he considered Ray's increasing interference. Ray had an extensive knowledge of and appreciation of Western music and wanted to use it in his films. He would later would claim that forms of Western art music like the sonata influenced the structure of his films and that Indian music, with its unfixed sense of time, chafed against the very construction of cinema itself.

Discussions with his composers were proving fruitless, and Ray found it easier to score his films himself. With no formal musical training, Ray turned his hand to composition, orchestration, and even conducting. Fulfilling the roles of both director and composer put Ray in a unique position. He would begin the composing process by conceiving of the key musical ideas as he wrote the screenplay and then developing those ideas throughout production. Ray would whistle the tunes initially, then pick them out on the piano, and notate them in Western notation. Ray began composing his own film scores in the late 1950s and continued to do so throughout his career.

Other directors have exerted a determining influence on the scores for their films. John Ford chose the songs in his westerns, the iconic folk tunes, period songs, and hymns that fill the soundtrack. Ford was a great student of US history and knew the music of the period, making many of the musical choices before a composer was even assigned to the film. This put some composers in the awkward position of having to ask Ford what songs he had chosen for their film scores. (But as we have seen, sometimes even Ford's choices were tampered with.)

Kurosawa also had very specific ideas when it came to the music. He actually gave his composers musical models to imitate: Ravel's *Bolero* for *Rashomon* (1950), Lizst's *Second Hungarian Rhapsody* for *Yojimbo* (1961) and *Sanjuro* (1962), Haydn's Symphony 101 (*The Clock*) and Beethoven's Ninth Symphony for *Red Beard* (1965), and Mahler's First Symphony for *Ran* (1985). Masaru Satô, who worked with Kurosawa on nine films, described Kurosawa's interest in the score as passionate. Satô revealed that they had thorough discussions of the music before filming began. But Kurosawa, as he did with other members of the crew, fought with his composers. Akira Ifukube scored *The Quiet Duel* (1949). Kurosawa gave him Juventino Rossi's "Over the Waves" as the musical model; Ifukube felt so compromised by the experience that he would not work for Kurosawa again. Takemitsu parted company with Kurosawa over what he felt was unwelcome interference. Even Fumio Hayasaka, whose untimely death devastated Kurosawa, fought with the director over being forced to imitate Ravel's *Bolero*. In all fairness, it should be noted that Kurosawa contended that he was not unwilling (sometimes) to compromise. When Hayasaka insisted on using a trumpet over his objections in *Scandal* (1950), Kurosawa admitted that Hayasaka was right. The trumpet is in the score.

Jean-Luc Godard, among film's most iconoclastic of filmmakers, had similarly iconoclastic ideas about the score. He didn't so much collaborate with his composers as utilize the music they produced in ways that he saw fit. He asked Michel Legrand to write a theme and variations for *Vivre sa vie* (1962) and then used only one out of the twelve variations, truncating its use by abruptly halting the music in mid-variation.

Collaborating with the director can give a composer a more active role. The relationship between Soviet director Sergei Eisenstein and composer Sergei Prokofiev is a case in point. On *Alexander Nevsky* (1938), Eisenstein involved Prokofiev from the beginning of the project. Prokofiev visited the set and regularly watched the dailies. According to Eisenstein, the two men would "bargain long and earnestly over 'which is to be the first'" and fought it out over whether it should be the music or the image. Sometimes Eisenstein won: Prokofiev would watch Eisenstein's edited footage, and Eisenstein would try to describe the nature of the shots so that Prokofiev could find a musical equivalent. Apparently Prokofiev was a quick study. He would go home after the meeting with Eisenstein and return the next day with the cue. Sometimes Prokofiev won: some of the score was composed and even recorded before the footage was edited, enabling Eisenstein to edit some sequences to the score.

All of these practices were exceptional in 1938 in the Soviet Union, and they would be exceptional today. Prokofiev was very savvy about recording, having visited Walt Disney's studio during the 1930s and been introduced to its state-of-the-art recording techniques. Of course, the technology at recording studios in the Soviet Union of 1938 was far from what Disney had. André Previn described Prokofiev's music for *Alexander Nevsky* as the greatest film score ever written on the worst soundtrack ever recorded, and Russell Merritt has described it as sounding like "a chamber ensemble recorded over a telephone." Prokofiev had about twenty musicians for the recording sessions, but he nonetheless managed some innovative solutions: using the distortions produced by placing instruments too close to the microphones to add disorienting effects to the villainous Teutonic knights; or placing the brasses far from the microphones to lessen their formidable associations; or scoring instruments in the extremes of their registers and manipulating their sound to produce the effect of ancient instruments. Prokofiev disliked quoting ancient music—he felt it would just sound alien to modern audiences—and instead composed his own medieval-sounding folk tunes.

Several other important composer-director collaborations around the world include Arthur Honegger and Abel Gance, Maurice Jaubert and Jean Vigo, Georges Auric and Jean Cocteau, and Pierre Jansen and Claude Chabrol in France; Shostakovich and Grigori Kozintsev in the Soviet Union; Hayasaka with both Kurosawa and Mizoguchi in Japan; Václav Trojan and Jiří Trnka in Czechoslovakia; Nino Rota and Federico Fellini and Morricone and Leone in Italy; Per Raben and Fassbinder and Popol Vuh and Werner Herzog in Germany; and Zhao Jiping and Zhang Yimou in the PRC.

It is a rare composer who could actually ignore the wishes of the director, but Bernard Herrmann was just such a composer. Belligerent, opinionated, but immensely talented, Herrmann publicly declared that "If you were to follow the taste of most directors, the music would be awful. They really have no taste at all. I'm overstating a bit, of course. There are exceptions....

Hitchcock is very sensitive: he leaves me alone!" The Herrmann-Hitchcock collaboration was one of the most famous in Hollywood, although given Herrmann's proclivities, collaboration might not be the right word to describe their relationship. Hitchcock had definite ideas about the music and a good intuitive sense of where music should go, often reflected in his detailed "Sound Notes." He usually involved himself in the production of the score, to a greater and greater degree as his career flourished. But he gave Herrmann plenty of room and came to depend on him. For the famous love scene in *Vertigo* (1958), when Judy emerges in the hotel room as Scotty's fantasy, an extended, dialogueless sequence, Hitchcock explained to Herrmann, "We'll just have the camera and you." On *Psycho* (1960), Hitchcock determined that the shower sequence didn't need music. According to Herrmann, Hitchcock told him, "Well, do what you like, but only one thing I ask of you: please write nothing for the murder in the shower." Herrmann, of course, did otherwise, producing one of the most arresting and imitated music cues in all of cinema.

Herrmann was generally involved from the beginning and attended preproduction meetings with Hitchcock, came and went on the set, offered suggestions not only about the score but about other aspects of the film, was consulted about the placement of music, and as we have seen, ignored Hitchcock's directives when he disagreed with them.

As the partnership continued, it began to sour and finally ended badly. Hitchcock was under pressure from the studio to use pop music in *Torn Curtain* (1966) and initially supported Herrmann's refusal to have anything to do with such commercial pressures. But, as usual, Herrmann ignored key Hitchcock directives about the music only to find out that this time, Hitchcock was having none of it. Herrmann was unceremoniously fired by Hitchcock after recording one cue of the score. (Hitchcock would later dump the score that Henry Mancini composed for *Frenzy* [1972],

9. One of the most famous collaborations between a composer and a director was the one between Bernard Herrmann and Alfred Hitchcock. Here, Hitchcock (*left*) and Herrmann are posed in a publicity shot on the set of *The Man Who Knew Too Much* (1956).

reportedly telling him that it sounded too much like Herrmann.) Once friends on set and off, Hitchcock and Herrmann never reconciled. In the 1970s Herrmann was discovered by New Hollywood, including Brian De Palma, for whom he scored *Obsession* (1976), and Martin Scorsese, for whom he scored *Taxi Driver* (1976). Herrmann died the night he finished conducting *Taxi Driver*. Hitchcock once credited Herrmann's music with 33 percent of the effect of *Psycho*. Herrmann revised that figure upward to 60 percent. What is not in dispute is the quality of these men's work together. In nine of Hitchcock's greatest films, Herrmann was able to give musical form to the unconscious fears and desires at the heart of Hitchcock, including *The Man Who Knew Too Much* (1956), *Vertigo, North by Northwest* (1959), and, of course, *Psycho.*

Takemitsu managed to sustain a working relationship with Kurosawa over the course of several films including *Ran* (1985), but it was a difficult partnership. Takemitsu, as Japan's most celebrated composer of art music, was used to directors ceding control to him. For the score for *Dodeskaden* (1970), however, Kurosawa wanted Takemitsu to use Bizet's *L'Arlésienne* as the musical prototype. When Takemitsu responded that if Kurosawa wanted Bizet, he should hire Bizet, Kurosawa, perhaps stunned by such unexpected insubordination, allowed Takemitsu to compose original music instead. On *Ran,* Kurosawa gave Takemitsu Mahler's First Symphony as a guide for the battle sequence. Takemitsu disagreed with the choice but found a unique strategy to go his own way. The score for the battle sequence is indeed Mahleresque with nods to the First Symphony, but it includes another Mahler piece that Kurosawa did not request, *Songs of the Earth.* If Kurosawa noticed Takemitsu's disobedience, he never said anything about it. Takemitsu and Kurosawa parted company, however, over this very issue. For *Rhapsody in August* (1991), Kurosawa wanted Takemitsu to incorporate the Schubert song "*Heidenröslein*" ("The Wild Rose") into the score, and Takemitsu walked away. "*Heidenröslein*" does appear prominently in the film. One presumes that score's composer, Shinichiro Ikebe, proved more accommodating.

The temp track

Often, and increasingly common in film production today, composers are faced with a temp track, a set of musical cues culled from existing musical literature and roughly synched up with the film. If you've seen previews of coming attractions in a movie theater recently, you've probably heard a temp track. For feature films, a temp track can be drawn from popular music, art music, or other film scores. Temp tracks are designed to provide models and, in the best case scenario, offer a form of aural communication between director and composer. A temp track has saved more than one film. For *The Graduate* (1967), director Mike Nichols chose Simon and Garfunkel to score the film with a series of new songs, thinking that their music was exactly what his film's protagonist would listen to. Nichols temp tracked the film with several existing Simon and Garfunkel songs. But Paul Simon encountered the musical version of writer's block and had only produced a few bars of "Mrs. Robinson" when editing was complete and the film was ready to be scored. Nichols, in desperation, ended up using the temp track to great acclaim and huge commercial success. In all fairness, Simon tells the story differently, claiming that Nichols rejected his newly composed songs in favor of the temp track. It wouldn't be the first time.

The temp track can be a kind of straitjacket, locking composers into imitating specific pieces of music. In the worst case, the examples it provides become so wedded to the film in the director's mind that no matter what original music the composer devises, it will never sound right. The most famous example of the tyranny of the temp track concerns *2001: A Space Odyssey* (1968), for which Stanley Kubrick culled a series of selections from his record collection including, famously, Richard Strauss's *Also Sprach Zarathustra*. Alex North composed an original score, but Kubrick decided that he liked his temp track better and without so much as telling North before the premiere, he discarded North's entire score. Plenty of art music finds its way into a film score through the temp track. Samuel Barber's *Adagio for Strings*, for instance, used in Oliver Stone's *Platoon* (1986), was on the temp track and was ultimately chosen over Georges Delerue's original theme.

The most indefinable part of film scoring comes next: composing. Film composers have a variety of explanations for how they find inspiration (or how they function when they don't), and they range from bolt-out-of-the-blue flashes of insight to disciplined craftsmanship. Anil Biswas, working in Bollywood in the 1930s, said that "Music must belong to the period and to the character [of the film], and that used to give me ideas when I sat to compose." Rachel Portman describes her experience in this way: "It can be something very small, like a four-note melodic chain or a movement from one chord to another, that you suddenly know is going to be the heart of the music, the language and the syntax for the entire film." Delerue describes his experience in quite another: "In reality you have to force yourself, you have to concentrate on things like a sportsman does. That's when the ideas arrive." Says Jerry Goldsmith: "We like to think it is all art, but let's face it, we have to rely on craft a lot of times." Morricone, who by his own count has composed more than 450 film scores, describes the process as part technique, part inspiration. Glass cautions against becoming too immersed in the film: "Composers want to know how to write music, how you get an idea, and I tell them—and they are a little surprised—don't look at the movie too much."

Federico Fellini asserted that he had an active hand in creating scores with longtime collaborator Nino Rota, describing how he would stand over Rota at the piano and tell him exactly what kind of music he wanted. Rota, however, tells the story a bit differently. A quick study and an exceptionally gifted improviser, Rota would compose multiple themes of his own ahead of time and play them for Fellini until he hit upon one that Fellini liked, giving Fellini the impression that he was inspiring Rota at the piano.

Composers may work at a desk, at a piano, or nowadays, at a computer keyboard. Aaron Copland composed at a piano while the film was projected. Some, like Morricone, compose conventionally with staff paper and a pencil; others, like Rahman, compose at a computer keyboard. Some work in complete isolation, and some like hubbub. They are all under the gun to produce musical ideas quickly.

Composers are largely able to do so, at least in large-scale production systems, such as Hollywood and Bollywood, because of a highly specific division of labor. In Hollywood, from the classical studio era to the present, composers generally sketch out their ideas, in varying degrees of specificity, and work with orchestrators, arrangers, and copyists who produce the final version of the score. This means that Hollywood composers rarely orchestrate their own music. (In the international film music community, however, composers tend to orchestrate their own work and as a result can have trouble adjusting to working in Hollywood.) It was not even uncommon in the classical studio era for one composer to work on several scores simultaneously or for several composers to work on one score simultaneously. In the latter case, multiple contributions were usually masked by the studio with a single composer receiving screen credit. *Stagecoach* (1939) is exceptional in this regard with five composers sharing screen credit and the Oscar that year. However, at least two other composers contributed to the score uncredited.

In Bollywood, before the advent of computer-driven score production in the 1990s, music directors would assemble teams for orchestrating, copying, conducting, and even composing the background score. In fact, before the end of the twentieth century, those who composed the background score often went uncredited and thus it was assumed, wrongly, that music directors were responsible for all the music in a film, not just the songs. There were even actual assembly lines to produce scores. Keyboardist Benny Rosario remembers the process: "Vincent [Alvarez] would mark the film, and then Anil [Paudwal] would write something for the first mark, and Vincent would copy it, and then Anil would record it, and while he was recording, Arun [Paudwal] would be writing something for the next mark, and again Vincent would copy, and then Arun would record, and Anil would be writing something. We never stopped." Of course, this meant keeping players at the ready throughout the scoring process, and composers established relationships with players they could depend upon to participate in this way.

Composers, especially those working in Hollywood, have learned to compensate for the fact that film scores are not produced by a single individual. Many composers create an elaborate sketch including not only melody and harmony but orchestration cues. John Barry, for instance, writes extremely detailed sketches on a twelve-stave score with harmonies and instrumentations, including all the solo parts, written out. Others, like James Horner, will fully orchestrate a few bars and leave the orchestrator to finish the cue. Still others establish a long-term relationship with an orchestrator or arranger who could be trusted to reproduce a composer's style: Korngold with Hugo Friedhofer (who became an important composer himself), Dimitri Tiomkin with choral arranger Jester Hairston, John Williams with Herbert Spencer, Elfman with fellow Oingo Boingo band member Steve Bartek.

The relationship of Elfman and Bartek illustrates some of the anxieties that still surround orchestration in Hollywood. Elfman and Bartek were members of the eclectic rock band Oingo Boingo, but when Elfman first began film scoring in the 1980s, he composed in the Romantic, symphonic style of the classical Hollywood film score. His *Batman* (1989) is clearly modeled after those of Korngold and Rózsa, Elfman's acknowledged influences. To this day, very few of Elfman's scores use pop music in any sustained way, and he has gone on record to express his dislike for pop scores.

Elfman has been completely candid about the contribution of Bartek. Writing in *Keyboard*, Elfman states, "I can write a fairly elaborate sketch—12, 14, or 16 staves of music—but I depend on my orchestrator, Steve Bartek, to put it into a legitimate context." Bartek confirms that Elfman "writes every note in the score," although he didn't exactly clarify things when he went on to describe Elfman's quirky musical notation: "He considers notation a problem for him, because [of]...dynamic markings....He's not good at bass clef,...His notation is not strictly normal, but for anybody who knows anything about notation, you can look at it and figure out what he's saying." Elfman has been saddled for years with the (mis)perception that he is a "hummer," in industry parlance, someone who can't actually write music, much less orchestrate, and who hums the melodies to others who realize the score. Janet Halfyard argues that Elfman's experience in Hollywood unmasks deeply buried prejudices in the musical community against film scoring, holding film composers up to standards of the concert hall still steeped in Romantic notions of the inviolate individual creativity of the artist and his or her unique production of a work of art.

Orchestrators also work on music that has been electronically produced. After the invention of MIDI, it was possible for composers to create sequencer files that record data and produce the musical notation necessary to play it. Orchestrators worked from these sequencer files. The new digital technology, at least at this point, does not produce notation for digitally recorded sound. Transcribers have to be called in to listen to the composer's music files, usually on a CD or MP3, and transcribe it the old-fashioned way, by ear, into conventional notation before an orchestrator can be called in.

Recording

The final component of a score's production is its recording. Many composers like to conduct their own scores, and some are in a position to do so. It is a job, however, that breeds fear in the heart of many a first-time film composer. Achieving precise synchronization between the music and the images, usually projected on a large screen behind the orchestra and visible to the conductor, is not easy. The lag time in perception between seeing an image and responding to it spurred the development of systems capable of assisting conductors and players in producing precise timing: the *click track*, an audible metronome delivered to the musicians via headphones; *punches* and *streamers*, actually holes punched and lines scratched into the film at strategic points so that the conductor is prepared for important moments of synchronization; and *free timing*, the use of a large stopwatch to facilitate precision. In the heyday of the Hollywood studio system, studios had large orchestras, anywhere from thirty-eight to sixty-five players under contract. Today, studios no longer have the luxury of keeping that many musicians on staff, but big-budget films can still command a huge orchestra: the score for *Batman* was recorded by 110 players, the score for *Dances with Wolves*, by 95. In Bollywood, there were reportedly 300 musicians in the studio for *Mela* (1999).

Not all recording sessions are devoted to recording a fully notated score, and music for film is captured in many other ways. Ray has described the recording session for *Pather Panchali* (1955) where Shankar and a small group of musicians improvised the score while watching the film in a recording studio over the course of eleven hours. (Shankar remembers it as four and a half.) Shankar had not even seen all of the film when the recording session was held. Director Louis Malle asked Miles Davis to score *Elevator to the Gallows* (1958), giving Davis one night in the studio to improvise a score to a series of sequences that Malle had preselected.

Mixing (adjusting sound levels after recording) and *dubbing* (adding all the various sound tracks to the edited film) are processes in which the composer usually is not involved. If a cue is eliminated, the dubbing stage is most likely where it will happen. Cues often end up on the cutting room floor unbeknownst to the composer. "I try and stay fairly calm about cues disappearing under cars," says James Newton Howard. "What are you going to do?" Leonard Bernstein remembers attending a dubbing session for *On the Waterfront* (1954) and watching in horror as a music cue that he felt was crucial to the film was virtually eliminated to accommodate Marlon Brando's grunt. Entire scores have even been jettisoned, famously Herrmann's for *Torn Curtain* and North's for *2001: A Space Odyssey*, less famously Mychael Danna's for *The Hulk* (2003), with Danna only days away from recording it.

The advent of technological innovations in sound production has had radical (some might argue liberating) consequences for film scoring and recording. It is theoretically possible now, in many parts of the world, for a composer to virtually create and produce an entire score, thus eliminating the need for teams of assistants, arrangers, and copyists to realize the score, and live musicians on acoustic instruments to perform it. In many film industries it is becoming increasingly necessary for composers to have computer expertise. In Bollywood, for instance, it has become so commonplace for scores to be digitally produced on a synthesizer that the very nomenclature has begun to change, with the term "programmer" replacing "music director." Such changes to film scoring have been so dramatic and the economic consequences so profound that Gregory Booth, in a recent book on the Mumbai film industry, labels the preprogramming years "Old Bollywood" and postprogramming "New Bollywood."

Although this chapter has been devoted to composers and their craft, sometimes composers have been prevented from practicing

A. R. Rahman

A. R. Rahman, born and raised in Madras (now Chennai) and educated at Oxford University, began his professional life as a musician writing jingles for television commercials. Credited with revolutionizing film scoring in his native India and catapulted into international prominence with his double Oscar win for score and song in *Slumdog Millionaire* (2008), Rahman stands at the forefront of change in film music. That change includes bringing the music of his native Tamil Nadu to his film scores, and with their success, heightened visibility for the Tamil film industry; increasing awareness in the international film community about Indian music (he is conversant in the musical styles—traditional, folk, and popular—of India's many distinct cultural regions); and transforming the process by which film scores are produced in India, introducing digital sampling and synthesized film scores (he composes on a Mac using Logic Studio software).

Rahman earned his first film commission for the Tamil film *Roja* (1992) by playing the director some of his music samples. He went on to score the film in an eclectic mix of Tamil folk and traditional music, reggae, African rhythms, lush violins and Romantic harmonies, and hints of Morricone's spaghetti western scores. Rahman later began scoring films in the Hindi industry the first of which, *Rangeela* (1995), was enormously popular. He is, at the moment, the most successful film composer in India, working on as many as five or six film scores a year. The soundtrack albums from his films have sold more copies than the Beatles. His international work includes the West End/ Broadway musical *Bombay Dreams* (2002) produced by Andrew Lloyd Webber, scores for the English-language film *Elizabeth: The Golden Age* (2007) (with Craig Armstrong), the Mandarin-language film *Warriors of Heaven and Earth* (2003), and, of course, the English/Hindi-language film *Slumdog Millionaire*. His eclectic style is a fusion of global influences: Indian music, especially the traditional and popular traditions of his native Tamil Nadu, Sufi Muslim chanting (in 1988 Rahman converted to Islam and adopted his present name), Bollywood disco beats, Asian musics, African rhythms, reggae, Western art music, and Western popular music, especially hip-hop, rap, and technopop. When asked if he believed in a universal music, he answered, "I do, because all of us are, in a way, getting multicultural in our ears."

10. A. R. Rahman was a double Oscar winner for Best Original Song ("Jai Ho") and Best Original Score for *Slumdog Millionaire* (2008).

their craft by political events—world wars, civil wars, cultural revolutions—and by intellectual and artistic repression. Maurice Jaubert lost his life in the defense of Paris in 1938. Korngold acknowledged that *The Adventures of Robin Hood* (1938) saved his life. A Jew, Korngold temporarily relocated to Hollywood in early 1938 to score the film for Warner Bros. but left his family behind in Vienna. When they were trapped by the Anschluss, the studio used its resources and influence to get them out of Austria. Korngold was convinced that had he not scored *Robin Hood*, he and his family would have perished in Nazi concentration camps.

The score for *Alexander Nevsky* did something close to saving Sergei Prokofiev's life in the Stalinist Soviet Union of the 1930s when artists, intellectuals, filmmakers, and composers feared for their lives (and many lost theirs, like Boris Shumyatsky, head of the Mosfilm film studio) when their ideas or their art did not pass muster with Soviet authorities. Prokofiev was under suspicion not only because he had recently returned from the West where he had been living but also because he employed Modernism in his music, not an idiom in favor with Communist Party officials. On his last concert tour of the West, Prokofiev was prevented from taking his wife and children, who were held in Moscow as a kind of collateral against his return. Eisenstein was also on thin ice with the party and had recently been pressured to apologize publicly for the wayward ideology in his *Bezhin Meadow* (1937), which was pulled from production. Later, Stalin personally attended a preview screening of *Alexander Nevsky*, which won his approval, protecting Eisenstein and Prokofiev, at least for the time being, from the fate that had befallen others who strayed from the party line. Other Modernist composers in the Soviet Union, notably Dmitri Shostakovich, whose concert music was officially denounced and banned, also found refuge in scoring films.

During the Cultural Revolution in the PRC, Western music was banned, as was traditional Chinese music of any kind including opera and folk music. Tan Dun found himself reassigned from music school in Beijing to a rice paddy in Hunan for two years. The Islamic Revolution in Iran initially cast a dark shadow over the lives of many Iranian composers who were effectively prevented from pursuing careers in the concert hall by prohibitions on public performances of their music. Many turned to film composing. In the United States, too, straying from the dominant ideology, or the mere appearance of doing so, could get you blacklisted during the McCarthy era, or if you weren't a citizen, deported. Hanns Eisler, a German émigré who had composed workers songs during the 1920s in Germany and who openly criticized capitalism, was forced to leave after hearings before HUAC in 1948, never to return to a country he loved or to a thriving Hollywood career. We like to think of music as somehow untouched by politics, a pure form of artistic expression, a direct form of access to the composer's soul, unencumbered and unfettered by worldly concerns. But as film composers' lives demonstrate, worldly concerns can indeed separate a composer from his or her craft.

Conclusion

Film music had its inception at the beginning of film history, and it continues to be part and parcel of film production today. Its practice has become virtually indispensable to the marketability of contemporary films throughout the world. Witness the insertion of several songs by jazz singer Dianne Reeves into the gritty realism of the recent *Good Night, and Good Luck* (2005), a film that otherwise omits musical accompaniment entirely. Cross-promoted on radio, television, and the Internet, and recorded and transmitted in various mediums, soundtracks featuring a film's music now precede a film's release and may produce higher profits than the film itself.

In some ways, film music has come full circle. The advent of the compilation score harkens back to silent film accompaniment with its cue sheets of specific musical references, many of which quote popular music and song. Musical accompaniment is one of the many ways in which film as an art form is returning to its roots in the late nineteenth and early twentieth century when Edison initially envisioned film viewing as an activity taking place in the home, an amalgamation of music and image experienced in the family parlor.

There are new frontiers, too. It is interesting to consider the presence and power of music in television, and to even newer media such as music videos, video games, and websites. How and why did music become crucial to the ways in which these phenomena operate at least some of the time? Music in film, after all, is functional; it provides very specific qualities to the medium, qualities that film has come to depend upon. To what extent do these new media forms depend upon music as well? What functions that music provides to film might also prove crucial in these new arenas? At this point, I am not prepared to offer even a "very short" answer. I will leave these and questions like them to others to answer. In doing so I hope that they will recognize the power of film music and chart its continuing legacy.

References

Chapter 1

Quentin Tarantino's first quote is from Gerald Peary, 46, and the second from Jeff Dawson, 81.

Chapter 2

A. R. Rahman is quoted in "10 Questions for A. R. Rahman" at *Time* online, 26 March 2009 (www.time.com/time/magazine/article/0,9171,1887759,00.html). John Barry is quoted in the documentary *Dances with Wolves: The Creation of an Epic*. Randy Newman is quoted in Fred Karlin's *Listening to the Movies: The Film Lover's Guide to Film Music* (New York: Schirmer, 1994), 72. The quote from Theodor Adorno and Hanns Eisler is from their *Composing for the Films*, 8. Claudia Gorbman's quotes come from her *Unheard Melodies: Narrative Film Music*, 16 and 58. Noël Carroll's quote comes from his *Mystifying Movies*: *Fads and Fallacies in Contemporary Film Theory*, 219. Elmer Bernstein is quoted in Tony Thomas's *The View from the Podium* (New York: A. S. Barnes, 1973), 193. Jerrold Levinson's quote come from his "Film Music and Narrative Agency," 272.

Chapter 3

Kurt London's work is drawn from his *Film Music,* trans. Eric S. Bensinger (London: Faber & Faber, 1936; reprint New York: Arno, 1970), especially "Illustration," 60–61, and "Aesthetics and psychology," 33–39. Jean Mitry's quote appears in "Music and Cinema," trans. William Frawley, *Film Reader* 4 (1979): 142.

Michel Chion's quotes appear in his *Audio-Vision: Sound on Screen*, 82 and 47. Claudia Gorbman's quotes appear in her *Unheard Melodies: Narrative Film Music*, 55, 58, and 64.

The material on Theodor Adorno's work is drawn largely from his *Introduction to the Sociology of Music*, trans. E. B. Ashton (New York: Seabury Press, 1976). The quotes from Theodor Adorno and Hanns Eisler are from their *Composing for the Films*, 59. The material from Jacques Attali is drawn from his *Noise: The Political Economy of Music,* trans. Brian Massumi (Minneapolis: University of Minnesota Press, 1985). The quotes from Caryl Flinn are from her *Strains of Utopia: Gender, Nostalgia, and Hollywood Film Music*, 9.

The quote "sonorous envelope of the self" is from Didier Anzieu in his "L'enveloppe sonore du soi," *Nouvelle revue de psychanalyse* 13 (Spring 1976): 161; "sonorous space" is a quote from Gérard Blanchard in his *Images de la musique de cinéma* (Paris: Edilig, 1984), 95; and "the murmuring house" is a quote from Guy Rosolato in his "La voix: entre corps et langage," *Revue francaise de psychanalyses* 38, no. 1 (January 1974): 81. Rosolato's second quote comes from the same source, 82. All translations from the French are my own. The quote from Daihachi Oguchi comes from the *Los Angeles Times*, 1 July 2008, B6. Ben Winters' quote comes from his "Corporeality, Musical Heartbeats, and Cinematic Emotion," *MSMI* (*Music Sound and the Moving Image*) 2, no. 1 (2008): 22.

Chapter 4

The quotes from Thomas Edison come from W. K. L. and Antonia Dickson's *History of the Kinetograph, Kinetoscope, and Kinetophonograph* (New York: Crowell, 1895; reprint New York: MOMA, 2002) and the *Montreal Daily Star* of 20 April 1895, reprinted in *Film History* 11, no. 4 (1999): 405. The quote from the Russian newspaper is reported by Yuri Tsivian in his *Early Cinema in Russia and Its Cultural Reception*, trans. Alan Bodger (London: Routledge, 1994), 229, n. 44. The quote from *Moving Picture News* comes from the edition of 19 March 1910.

Chapter 5

Scott Bradley's quote appears in his "Music in Cartoons" in *The Cartoon Music Book*, 118.

Chapter 6

Tôru Takemitsu's quote is from Donald Richie's "Notes on the Film Music of Takemitsu Tôru," *Contemporary Music Review* 21, no. 4 (2002): 10.

Satyajit Ray's quote is from his *Our Films, Their Films* (New York: Hyperion, 1994), 73. Mervyn Cooke's quote appears in his *A History of Film Music*, 507. Tan Dun's quote is from *New York Times* online (www.nytimes.com/2008/05/04/magazine/04dun-t.html). Alberto Iglesias's quote is from Kathleen M. Vernon and Cliff Eisen's "Contemporary Spanish Film Music: Carlos Saura and Pedro Almodóvar," in *European Film Music*, 51. Hamid Naficy's position is drawn largely from his "Islamizing Film Culture in Iran" in *Political Culture in the Islamic Republic*, ed. Samih K. Farsoun and Mehrdad Mashayekhi (London: Routledge, 1992), 178–213.

Chapter 7

Bernard Herrmann's quotes, with one exception, come from his 1973 address, "The Coming of Sound to American Film," reprinted in *Sound and the Cinema*, ed. Evan William Cameron (Pleasantville, NY: Redgrave, 1980), 121 and 132. The remaining Herrmann quote comes from George Burt, *The Art of Film Music* (Boston: Northeastern University Press, 1994), 221.

Max Steiner's quote comes from his "The Music Director," in *The Real Tinsel*, ed. Bernard Rosenberg and Harry Silverstein (London: Macmillan, 1970), 392. The quote from Liu Zhuang comes from "Liu Zhuang: Composer" in *Chinese Film: The State of the Art in the People's Republic*, ed. George Stephen Semsel (New York: Praeger, 1987), 176–77. Quotes from James Newton Howard and John Corigliano come from Michael Schelle's *The Score: Interviews with Film Composers*, 22, 183, and 169. The John Barry quotes come from Michael Schelle's *The Score: Interviews with Film Composers*, 22, and the documentary *Dances with Wolves: The Creation of an Epic*, which also contains Kevin Costner's quote. The Ennio Morricone quotes come from his "A Composer Behind the Film Camera," trans. Elena Boschi, in *MSMI (Music, Sound, and the Moving Image)* 1, no. 1 (2007): 98 and 97.

Miklós Rózsa's first quote comes from Royal S. Brown, *Overtones and Undertones: Reading Film Music* (Berkeley: University of California Press, 1993), 272, and the remaining quotes from his autobiography, *A Double Life* (New York: Hippocrene, 1982), 98 and 126. The Philip Glass quotes come from "Variations on the Musical Image: An Interview with Philip Glass," conducted by James Tobias in *Documentary Box*, no. 22 (2003), 23. Sergei Eisenstein's quote comes from his *Notes of a Film Director*, trans. X. Danko (New York: Dover, 1970), 156. The André Previn and Russell Merritt quotes come from Merritt's "Recharging Nevsky: Tracking the Eisenstein-Prokofiev War

Horse," *Film Quarterly* 48, no. 2 (Winter 1994–95): 44. The Hitchcock quote comes from Steven C. Smith's *A Heart at Fire's Center* (Berkeley: University of California Press, 1991), 222. The quote from Paul Thomas Anderson comes from "There Will Be Music" in *Entertainment Weekly* online (www.ew.com/ew/article/0,,20155516_20155530_20158721,00.html). The quotes from Shankar Indorkar, Anil Biswas, and Benny Rosario come from Gregory D. Booth's *Behind the Curtain: Making Music in Mumbai's Film Studios*, 157, 261, and 201. The quotes from Rachel Portman, Georges Delerue, and Jerry Goldsmith can be found in Fred Karlin's *Listening to the Movies: The Film Lover's Guide to Film Music*, 27 and 28.

The quotes from Danny Elfman and Steve Bartek appear in Janet K. Halfyard's *Danny Elfman's Batman: A Film Score Guide*, 12, 15, and 14. The A. R. Rahman quotes appear in "10 Questions for A. R. Rahman" in *Time* online, 26 March 2009 (www.time.com/time/magazine/article/0,9171,1887759,00.html); "Scoring *Slumdog Millionaire* with Logic: An Interview with A. R. Rahman," Apple online (www.apple.com/logicstudio/action/arrahman/); and "A. R. Rahman, *Slumdog Millionaire* Maestro," *Time* online, 5 February 2009 (www.time.com/time/arts/article/0,8599,1876545,00.html).

Further reading

Chapter 1

Chanko, Kenneth. "It's Got a Nice Beat, You Can Torture to It." *New York Times*. 20 February 1994, sec. 2, 19.

Dawson, Jeff. *Quentin Tarantino: The Cinema of Cool*. New York: Applause, 1995.

Garner, Ken. "'Would You Like to Hear Some Music?': Music In-and-out-of-control in the Films of Quentin Tarantino." In *Film Music: Critical Approaches*, edited by K. J. Donnelly, 188–205. New York: Continuum, 2001.

Peary, Gerald, ed. *Quentin Tarantino: Interviews*. Jackson: University of Mississippi Press, 1998.

Chapter 2

Adorno, Theodor (uncredited in the original English-language edition), and Hanns Eisler, *Composing for the Films*. New York: Oxford University Press, 1947; reprint London: Athlone Press, 1994.

Carroll, Noël. "A Contribution to the Theory of Movie Music." In *Mystifying Movies: Fads and Fallacies in Contemporary Film Theory*, 213–25. New York: Columbia University Press, 1988.

Chell, Samuel. "Music and Emotion in the Classical Hollywood Film: The Case of *The Best Years of Our Lives*." *Film Criticism* 8, no. 2 (Winter 1984): 27–38.

Frith, Simon. "Where Do Sounds Come From?" In *Performing Rights: On the Value of Popular Music*, 99–122. Cambridge, MA: Harvard University Press, 1996.

Gorbman, Claudia. *Unheard Melodies: Narrative Film Music.* Bloomington: Indiana University Press, 1987.

Kalinak, Kathryn. *Settling the Score: Music and the Classical Hollywood Film Score.* Madison: University of Wisconsin Press, 1992.

Larsen, Peter. "Musical Meanings." In *Film Music,* 66–75. London: Reaktion Books, 2005.

Levinson, Jerrold. "Film Music and Narrative Agency." In *Post-Theory: Reconstructing Film Studies,* edited by David Bordwell and Noël Carroll, 249–82. Madison: University of Wisconsin Press, 1996.

Neumeyer, David, and James Buhler, "Analytical and Interpretive Approaches to Film Music (I): Analysing the Music" and "Analytical and Interpretive Approaches to Film Music (II): Analysing Interactions of Music and Film." In *Film Music: Critical Approaches,* edited by K. J. Donnelly, 16–61. New York: Continuum, 2001.

Chapter 3

Adorno, Theodor, and Hanns Eisler, *Composing for the Films.* New York: Oxford University Press, 1947; reprint London: Athlone Press, 1994.

Attali, Jacques. *Noise: The Political Economy of Music.* Translated by Brian Massumi. Minneapolis: University of Minnesota Press, 1985.

Buhler, James, Caryl Flinn, and David Neumeyer, eds., *Music and Cinema.* Hanover, NH: University Press of New England, 2000.

Chion, Michel. *Audio-Vision: Sound on Screen.* Edited and translated by Claudia Gorbman. New York: Columbia University Press, 1994.

Flinn, Caryl. "'The Most Romantic Art of All': Music in the Classical Hollywood Film." *Cinema Journal* 29, no. 4 (Summer 1990): 35–50.

_____. *The New German Cinema: Music, History, and the Matter of Style.* Berkeley: University of California Press, 2004.

_____. "The 'Problem' of Femininity in Theories of Film Music." *Screen* 27, no. 6 (November–December 1986): 56–73.

_____. *Strains of Utopia: Gender, Nostalgia, and Hollywood Film Music.* Princeton, NJ: Princeton University Press, 1992.

Gabbard, Krin. *Jammin' at the Margins: Jazz and the American Cinema.* Chicago: University of Chicago Press, 1996.

Gorbman, Claudia. *Unheard Melodies: Narrative Film Music.* Bloomington: Indiana University Press, 1987.

Kalinak, Kathryn. "The Fallen Woman and the Virtuous Wife: Musical Stereotypes in *The Informer, Gone With the Wind,* and *Laura,*" *Film Reader* no. 5 (1981): 76–82.

——. *How the West Was Sung: Music in the Westerns of John Ford.* Berkeley: University of California Press, 2007.

Kassabian, Anahid. *Hearing Film: Tracking Identifications in Contemporary Hollywood Film Music.* New York: Routledge, 2001.

Smith, Jeff. "Unheard Melodies? A Critique of Psychoanalytic Theories of Film Music." In *Post-Theory: Reconstructing Film Studies,* edited by David Bordwell and Noël Carroll, 230–47. Madison: University of Wisconsin Press, 1996.

Wojcik, Pamela Robinson, and Arthur Knight, eds., *Soundtrack Available: Essays on Film and Popular Music.* Durham, NC: Duke University Press, 2001.

Chapter 4

Abel, Richard, and Rick Altman, eds. *The Sounds of Early Cinema.* Bloomington: Indiana University Press, 2001.

Altman, Rick. *Silent Film Sound.* New York: Columbia University Press, 2004.

Anderson, Gillian B. *Music for Silent Films, 1894–1929: A Guide.* Washington, DC: Library of Congress, 1988.

Carbine, Mary. "'The Finest Outside the Loop': Motion Picture Exhibition in Chicago's Black Metropolis, 1905–1928." In *Silent Film,* edited by Richard Abel, 234–62. New Brunswick, NJ: Rutgers University Press, 1996.

Cooke, Mervyn. "The 'Silent' Cinema." In *A History of Film Music,* 1–41. Cambridge: Cambridge University Press, 2008.

Film History. An International Journal. Vol. 1 (1987)—The Present. See especially 14, no. 1 (2002): Special Issue on Film Music.

Gallez, Douglas W. "Satie's *Entr'acte*: A Model of Film Music." *Cinema Journal* 16, no. 1 (Autumn 1976): 36–50.

Marks, Martin. *Music and the Silent Film: Contexts and Case Studies, 1895–1924.* New York: Oxford University Press, 1997.

Ogihara, Junka. "The Exhibition of Films of Japanese Americans in Los Angeles During the Silent Film Era." *Film History* 42, no. 2 (1990): 81–87.

Rapee, Erno. *Motion Picture Moods for Pianists and Organists.* New York: Schirmer, 1924; reprint New York: Arno, 1970.

———. *Encyclopedia of Music for Pictures*. New York: Belwin, 1925; reprint New York: Arno, 1970.

Robinson, David. "Music of the Shadows: The Use of Musical Accompaniment with Silent Films, 1896–1936." *Le giornate del cinema muto. Supplemento a Griffithiana*, no. 38/39 (October 1990): 1–19.

Tsivian, Yuri. "The acoustics of cinema performance." In *Early Cinema in Russia and Its Cultural Reception*, edited by Richard Taylor and translated by Alan Bodger, 65–84. London: Routledge, 1994.

Wierzbicki, James. "Music and the 'Silent' Film: (1894–1927)." In *Film Music: A History*, 13–68. New York: Routledge, 2009.

Zamecnik, J. S. *Sam Fox Moving Picture Music*, Vol. 1. Cleveland: Sam Fox Publishing, 1913.

Chapter 5

Cooke, Mervyn. *A History of Film Music*. Cambridge: Cambridge University Press, 2008.

Creekmur, Corey K. "Picturizing American Cinema: Hindi Film Songs and the Last Days of Genre." In *Soundtrack Available: Essays on Film and Popular Music*, edited by Pamela Robertson Wojcik and Arthur Knight, 375–406. Durham, NC: Duke University Press, 2001.

Egorova, Tatiana K. *Soviet Film Music: An Historical Survey*. Translated by Tatiana A. Ganf and Natalia A. Egunova. Amsterdam: Harwood Academic Publishers, 1997.

Farquhar, Mary, and Chris Berry. "Shadow Opera: Towards a New Archeology of the Chinese Cinema." In *Chinese-Language Film: Historiography, Poetics, Politics*, edited by Sheldon H. Lu and Emilie (Yueh-yu) Yeh, 27–51. Honolulu: University of Hawaii Press, 2005.

Flinn, Caryl. *Strains of Utopia: Gender, Nostalgia and Hollywood Film Music*. Princeton, NJ: Princeton University Press, 1992.

Gabbard, Krin. *Jammin' at the Margins: Jazz and the American Cinema*. Chicago: University of Chicago Press, 1996.

Goldmark, Daniel, and Yuval Taylor. *The Cartoon Music Book*. Chicago: A Cappella Press, 2002.

Kalinak, Kathryn. *Settling the Score: Music and the Classical Hollywood Film*. Madison: University of Wisconsin Press, 1992.

Mera, Miguel, and David Burnand, eds. *European Film Music*. Aldershot, England: Ashgate, 2006.

Rajadhyaksha, Ashish, and Paul Willemen, eds. *The Encyclopedia of Indian Cinema*. New York: Oxford University Press, 1995.

Shafik, Viola. "Music." In *Arab Cinema: History and Cultural Identity*. Cairo: American University in Cairo Press, 1998; rev. ed., 2007.

Stilwell, Robynn J., and Phil Powrie. *Composing for the Screen in Germany and the USSR*. Bloomington: Indiana University Press, 2008.

Tuohy, Sue. "Metropolitan Sounds: Music in Chinese Films of the 1930s." In *Cinema and Urban Culture in Shanghai, 1922–1943*, edited by Yingjin Zhang, 200–21. Palo Alto, CA: Stanford University Press, 1999.

Winters, Ben. *Erich Wolfgang Korngold's The Adventures of Robin Hood: A Film Score Guide*. Lanham, MD: Scarecrow Press, 2007.

Wierzbicki, James. "Music and the Early Sound Film: 1894–1933" and "Music in the 'Classical-Style' Hollywood Film (1933–1960)." In *Film Music: A History*, 69–130; 131–86. New York: Routledge, 2009.

Yeh, Emilie (Yueh-yu). "Historiography and Sinification: Music in Chinese Cinema of the 1930s." *Cinema Journal* 41, no. 3 (Spring 2002): 78–97.

Chapter 6

Booth, Gregory. *Behind the Curtain: Making Music in Mumbai's Film Studios*. New York: Oxford University Press, 2008.

Bruce, Graham. "Alma Brasileira: Music in the Films of Glauber Rocha." In *Brazilian Cinema*, edited by Randal Johnson and Robert Stam, 290–305. Rutherford, NJ: Fairleigh Dickinson University Press, 1982.

Cooke, Mervyn. *A History of Film Music*. Cambridge: Cambridge University Press, 2008.

Davison, Annette. *Hollywood Theory, Non-Hollywood Practice: Cinema Soundtracks in the 1980s and 1990s*. Aldershot, England: Ashgate, 2004.

Flinn, Caryl. *The New German Cinema: Music, History, and the Matter of Style*. Berkeley: University of California Press, 2004.

Hu, Brian, "The KTV Aesthetic: Popular Music Culture and Contemporary Hong Kong Cinema," *Screen* 47, no. 4 (Winter 2006): 407–24.

Kassabian, Anahid. *Hearing Film: Tracking Identifications in Contemporary Hollywood Film Music*. New York: Routledge, 2001.

Mera, Miguel, and David Burnand, eds. *European Film Music*. Aldershot, England: Ashgate, 2006.

MSMI: Music, Sound, and the Moving Image. Vol. 1, no. 1 (2007)—The Present.

Romney, Jonathan, and Adrian Wooton, eds. *Celluloid Jukebox: Popular Music and the Movies Since the 50s*. London: British Film Institute, 1995.

Slobin, Mark, ed. *Global Soundtracks: Worlds of Film Music*. Middletown, CT: Wesleyan University Press, 2008.

Smith, Jeff. *The Sounds of Commerce: Marketing Popular Film Music*. New York: Columbia University Press, 1998.

Wojcik, Pamela Robertson, and Arthur Knight, eds. *Soundtrack Available: Essays on Film and Popular Music*. Durham, NC: Duke University Press, 2001.

Yeh, Emilie (Yueh-yu). "A Life of Its Own: Musical Discourses in Wong Kar-wai's Films." *Post Script* 19, no. 1 (Fall 1999): 120–36.

Chapter 7

Booth, Gregory D. *Behind the Curtain: Making Music in Mumbai's Film Studios*. New York: Oxford University Press, 2008.

Brown, Royal S. "Herrmann, Hitchcock, and the Music of the Irrational." *Cinema Journal* 21, no. 2 (Spring 1982): 14–49; reprinted in *Overtones and Undertones: Reading Film Music*, 148–74. Berkeley: University of California Press, 1993.

The Cue Sheet: *Quarterly Journal of the Film Music Society*. Vol. 1, no. 1 (January 1984)—The Present.

Halfyard, Janet K. *Danny Elfman's Batman: A Film Score Guide*. Lanham, MD: Scarecrow Press, 2004.

Kalinak, Kathryn. *How the West Was Sung: Music in the Westerns of John Ford*. Berkeley: University of California Press, 2007.

Karlin, Fred. *Listening to the Movies: The Film Lover's Guide to Film Music*. New York: Schirmer, 1994.

Laing, Heather. *Gabriel Yared's The English Patient: A Film Score Guide*. Lanham, MD: Scarecrow Press, 2004.

Leinberger, Charles. *Ennio Morricone's The Good, the Bad, and the Ugly: A Film Score Guide*. Lanham, MD: Scarecrow Press, 2004.

Mera, Miguel. *Mychael Danna's The Ice Storm: A Film Score Guide*. Lanham, MD: Scarecrow Press, 2007.

Ray, Satyajit. "Music." *Satyajit Ray: An Anthology of Statements on Ray and By Ray*. New Delhi: Directorate of Film Festivals, Ministry of Information and Broadcasting, 1981.

Rózsa, Miklós. *Double Life: The Autobiography of Miklós Rózsa*. New York: Hippocrene Books, 1982.

Schelle, Michael. *The Score: Interviews with Film Composers*. Beverly Hills: Silman James Press, 1999.

Smith, Stephen C. *A Heart at Fire's Center*. Berkeley: University of California Press, 1991.

Sullivan, Jack. *Hitchcock's Music*. New Haven, CT: Yale University Press, 2006.

Winters, Ben. *Erich Wolfgang Korngold's The Adventures of Robin Hood: A Film Score Guide*. Lanham, MD: Scarecrow Press, 2007.

Recommended viewing

Chapter 1

Reservoir Dogs. 1992. Directed by Quentin Tarantino. Music Supervision by Karyn Rachtman.

Chapter 2

Beauty and the Beast. 1991. Directed by Gary Trousdale and Kirk Wise. Songs by Howard Ashman and Alan Menken. Score by Menken.

The Good, the Bad, and the Ugly. 1966. Directed by Sergio Leone. Score by Ennio Morricone.

Monsoon Wedding. 2001. Directed by Mira Nair. Score by Mychael Danna.

Psycho. 1960. Directed by Alfred Hitchcock. Score by Bernard Herrmann.

Chapter 4

Battleship Potemkin. 1925. Directed by Sergei Eisenstein. Original score by Edmund Meisel for the Berlin premiere. Kino International reissue with Mesiel's score.

Body and Soul. 1925. Directed by Oscar Micheaux. Criterion Collection reissue with new score by Wycliffe Gordon.

Broken Blossoms. 1919. Directed by D. W. Griffith. Original score by Louis F. Gottschalk. Kino International reissue with new score by Joseph Turrin.

Cabiria. 1914. Directed by Giovanni Pastrone. Score by Manlio Mazza. Kino International reissue with piano reduction of Mazza's score.

Entr-acte. 1924. Directed by Rene Clair. Score by Eric Satie. Criterion Collection reissue (together with *À nous la liberté* with score by Georges Auric).

La Roue. 1923. Directed by Abel Gance. Original score by Arthur Honegger. Flicker Alley reissue with new score by Robert Israel.

The Man with a Movie Camera. 1929. Directed by Dziga Vertov. Original score recreated by the Alloy Orchestra for the Pordenone Silent Film Festival premiere. Kino International reissue with new score by Michael Nyman.

Metropolis. 1927. Directed by Fritz Lang. Score by Gottfried Huppertz. Kino International reissue with score by Huppertz.

Napoleon. 1929. Directed by Abel Gance. Original score by Arthur Honegger. Zoetrope Studio reissue with a new score by Carmine Coppola.

The New Babylon. 1929. Director by Grigori Kozintsev and Leonid Trauberg. Original score by Dmitri Shostakovich. Eccentric Press (London) reissue with score by Shostakovich.

Nosferatu. 1922. Directed by F. W. Murnau. Score by Hans Erdmann. Kino International reissue, *Nosferatu: Ultimate Edition*, with score by Erdmann.

Sherlock Jr. 1924. Directed by Buster Keaton. Original score unknown. Kino International reissue (together with *Our Hospitality*) with new score by Clubfoot Orchestra.

The Thief of Bagdad. 1924. Directed by Raoul Walsh. Original score by Mortimer Wilson. Kino International reissue with a score adapted from the original cue sheet.

Chapter 5

The Adventures of Robin Hood. 1938. Directed by Michael Curtiz and William Keighley. Score by Erich Wolfgang Korngold.

Awara. 1951. Directed by Raj Kapoor. Music direction by Shankar-Jaikishan (Shankar Raghuwanshi and Jaikishan Pankal).

The Bad Sleep Well. 1960. Directed by Akira Kurosawa. Score by Masuro Satô.

The Cobweb. 1955. Directed by Vincente Minnelli. Score by Leonard Rosenman.

Deserter. 1934. Directed by Vsevolod Pudovkin. Score by Yuri Shaporin.

Elevator to the Gallows. 1958. Directed by Louis Malle. Score by Miles Davis.

The Jazz Singer. 1927. Directed by Alan Crosland. Score by Louis Silvers.

Kwaidan. 1965. Directed by Masaki Kobayashi. Score by Tŏru Takemitsu.

Le million. 1931. Directed by Rene Clair. Score by Armand Bernard, Philippe Parès, and Georges Van Parys.

Let's Go with Pancho Villa! 1936. Directed by Fernando de Fuentes. Score by Silvestre Revueltas.

Steamboat Willie. 1928. Produced by Walt Disney. Score uncredited.

Stray Dog. 1949. Directed by Akira Kurosawa. Score by Fumio Hayasaka.

Street Angel. 1937. Directed by Muzhi Yuan. Score by Luting He.

The Thin Blue Line. 1988. Directed by Errol Morris. Score by Philip Glass.

Chapter 6

Aguirre: The Wrath of God. 1972. Directed by Werner Herzog. Score by Popol Vuh.

Apu Trilogy. Directed by Satyajit Ray. Scores by Ravi Shankar. *Pather Panchali*. 1955. *Aparajito*. 1956. *The World of Apu*. 1960.

Black God, White Devil. 1964. Directed by Glauber Rocha. Score by Sérgio Ricardo.

Bladerunner. 1982. Directed by Ridley Scott. Score by Vangelis.

Chungking Express. 1994. Directed by Wong Kar-Wai. Original music by Fan-kai Chan, Michael Galasso, and Roel A. Garcia.

Crouching Tiger, Hidden Dragon. Directed by Ang Lee. Score by Tan Dun.

The English Patient. 1996. Directed by Anthony Minghella. Score by Gabriel Yared.

The Good, the Bad, and the Ugly. 1966. Directed by Sergio Leone. Score by Ennio Morricone.

Hamlet. 1964. Directed by Gregori Kosintsev. Score by Dmitri Shostakovich.

Half Moon. 2006. Directed by Bahman Ghobadi. Score by Hossein Alizadeh.

A Hard Day's Night. 1964. Directed by Richard Lester. Music direction by George Martin.

The Kite Runner. 2007. Directed by Marc Forster. Score by Alberto Iglesias.

Rashomon. 1950. Directed by Akira Kurosawa. Score by Fumio Hayasaka.

Star Wars trilogy. Scores by John Williams. *Star Wars*. 1977. Directed by George Lucas. *The Empire Strikes Back*. 1980. Directed by Irvin Kershner. *Return of the Jedi*. 1983. Directed by Richard Marquand.

Vivre sa vie. 1962. Directed by Jean-Luc Godard. Score by Michel Legrand.

Chapter 7

Alexander Nevsky. 1938. Directed by Sergei Eisenstein. Score by Sergei Prokofiev.

Batman. 1989. Directed by Tim Burton. Score by Danny Elfman.

Dances with Wolves. 1990. Directed by Kevin Costner. Score by John Barry.

Mahanagar. 1963. Directed by Satyajit Ray. Score by Ray.

My Darling Clementine. 1946. Directed by John Ford. Score by Cyril Mockridge.

On the Waterfront. 1954. Directed by Elia Kazan. Score by Leonard Bernstein.

Possession. 2002. Directed by Neil LaBute. Score by Gabriel Yared.

Ran. 1985. Directed by Akira Kurosawa. Score by Tôru Takemitsu.

Slumdog Millionaire. 2008. Directed by Danny Boyle. Score by A. R. Rahman.

Spellbound. 1945. Directed by Alfred Hitchcock. Score by Miklós Rózsa.

Taxi Driver. 1976. Directed by Martin Scorsese. Score by Bernard Herrmann.

There Will Be Blood. 2007. Directed by Paul Thomas Anderson. Score by Jonny Greenwood.

2001: A Space Odyssey. 1968. Directed by Stanley Kubrick. Score uncredited.

Vertigo. 1958. Directed by Alfred Hitchcock. Score by Bernard Herrmann.

Index

A

B

C

D

G

H

Q

R

S

T

U

V

W

Y

Z

short introduction

Patricia Aufderheide

In this concise, crisply written guide, Patricia Aufderheide takes readers along the diverse paths of documentary history and charts the lively, often fierce debates among filmmakers and scholars about the best ways to represent reality and to tell the truths worth telling. Drawing on the author's four decades of experience as a film scholar and critic, this book is the perfect introduction not just for teachers and students but also for all thoughtful filmgoers and for those who aspire to make documentaries themselves.

"This is probably the best general and most concise introduction to documentary that has been written to date . . . scholarship at its best."

Cahal McLaughlin, Senior Lecturer in Media Studies, School of Media, Film & Journalism, University of Ulster

ISBN 978-0-19-518270-5